The Evolving Virtual Library:

Visions and Case Studies

Edited by Laverna M. Saunders

Information Today, Inc.

Medford, NJ
1996

Copyright © 1996 by   Information Today, Inc.
143 Old Marlton Pike
Medford, NJ 08055

Printed in the United States of America

Library of Congress Cataloging-in-Publication Data

The evolving virtual library : visions and case studies / edited by
Laverna M. Saunders.
  p.   cm.
  Volume developed from a session of the Eighth Annual Computers in
Libraries Conference.
  Includes bibliographical references and index.
  ISBN 1-57387-013-7 (hardcover: alk. paper)
  1. Libraries—United States—Automation—Congresses.   2. Online
information services—United States—Congresses.   3. Library
information networks—United States—Congresses.   4. Digital
libraries—United States—Congresses.   I. Saunders, Laverna M.
II. Computers in Libraries Conference (8th : 1993 : Washington.
D.C.)
Z678.A4U633   1995
025´.00285—dc20   95-39544
                                                                            CIP

Price: $39.50

Managing Editor: Michelle A. Sutton-Kerchner
Cover Design: Jeanne Wachter

Contents

Editor's Preface

A transformation is taking place in all types of libraries. Just a few years ago, libraries were occupied primarily with developing local automated systems and collections of print materials. Although these functions are still being performed, external forces have created the need for change. Budget cutbacks and the escalating cost of materials, especially scholarly journals, have caused librarians to examine more carefully the collection needs of their users. The concept of access to remote resources which supplement or substitute for items owned locally has become more acceptable due to the availability of worldwide telecommunications networks, appropriate hardware and software, and machine-readable databases. The virtual library is the phenomenon of the international system of electronic networks which enable a user at a computer terminal to search bibliographic citations, databases, electronic publications, and other types of information in digital format. Synonyms for the virtual library include electronic library or library without walls.

The chapters contained in this volume address many of the practical issues involved in developing the *virtual library*. This evolutionary process is happening through scattered pilot projects which may serve as models for others. For the most part, these innovative projects are taking place at research universities where grant funding and/or adequate computing resources are available. However, public libraries and schools are also experimenting and providing telecommunications access.

A full-day session at the Eighth Annual Computers in Libraries Conference was devoted to "The Evolving Virtual Library: Visions and Case Studies." Although attendees came to learn about the pioneering projects described in this book, they were also challenged to determine their own role in creating the virtual library. The presentations from the conference are included in this volume in augmented form. The chapters on BUBL and network-based electronic journals and publishing have been added to provide further examples on an international level.

Saunders and Mitchell have supplemented the conference papers with a review of some of the landmark pilot projects which have developed during the first half of the decade. They trace the use of the term virtual library and various applications in academic libraries. In addition, they look at the impact of the Internet on the K-12 realm and how instruction at all levels is changing. They conclude their chapter with a vision of the future virtual library information system.

Connie Stout demonstrates in her chapter on the Texas Education Network (TENET), that K-12 educators in Texas are actively involved in networking. TENET offers a variety of services for educators, including electronic mail, news and conferencing, access to databases, and full Internet capabilities. Stout describes the investigative and decision-making steps used by the Texas Education Agency in establishing TENET. The process began with the State Board of Education's recommendation and subsequent legislative action which authorized the creation of an electronic information transfer system. The Texas Education Agency addressed numerous barriers, such as the lack of phone lines and computer equipment, and identified requirements for telecommunications services, which were met by The University of Texas System. Training in the use of the network, conference moderation, and curriculum integration has been incorporated into staff development courses. Testimonials by TENET users reveal how telecommunications can bring together students, teachers, and members of the community.

The Pikes Peak Library District is a public library dealing with a paradox. As Bernard Margolis explains, there is a tension between providing a virtual library environment and meeting increased user demands for services, facilities, and reading materials. Pikes Peak Library District has responded to patron interest and demands by developing a computer system called MAGGIE'S PLACE. Accessible 24 hours a day and available for free to all, MAGGIE'S PLACE receives an average of 5,000 calls each month. Through the Colorado Alliance of Research Libraries, and the network of other libraries participating with CARL, patrons have access to an entire universe of library catalogs. In addition, the library provides commercial online reference sources, and library staff create and maintain numerous local databases and indexes. The Pikes Peak Library District has dealt with the paradox by offering a superior book collection while simultaneously providing timeless and placeless access to thousands of people who might not be able to easily enter through a library's doors.

Providing full-text access through its second-generation information system is one of Carnegie Mellon University's goals. In her chapter, Barbara Richards elaborates on the vision and operating systems behind Project Mercury, which integrates library resources into the campus network infrastructure. This pilot project is a model of collaboration between librarians and computing professionals. It has also received grant funding from commercial information vendors such as OCLC, UMI, Elsevier, and IEEE, who are partners in developing specifications for electronic information. Carnegie Mellon is using client-server architecture for distributed storage and retrieval and is scanning sci-tech journal articles into digital format. In addition to listing design issues and how the project team approached them, Richards uses screen displays to illustrate how the system appears to users.

Public universities have an opportunity to take a leadership role in offering wide-scale access to the Internet, and George Machovec describes how Arizona State University (ASU) has seized the initiative. Accessing the worldwide Internet through a regional network called WESTNET, ASU serves as a regional node to all institutions and individuals in central and northern Arizona requiring access to the Internet. Machovec explores the issues which have to be considered in offering broad public and institutional access to the Internet. He also describes how the University Libraries at ASU provide transparent connectivity through the CARL system to remote systems as MELVYL (University of California), the Maricopa County Community Colleges system (a DRA system which runs ten community colleges in the Phoenix metropolitan area), and Phoenix Public Library (a CLSI system). The ASU Libraries have also begun a virtual library demonstration project in which librarians, faculty, and experts from Information Technology (the computer center) may jointly explore and develop cutting edge projects and products.

The growing range of resources and services available on national and international networks are of increasing importance to education and research efforts. Finding these resources and figuring out how to use them is still a major challenge. Dennis Nicholson's chapter on BUBL, the BUlletin Board for Libraries on JANET (the Joint Academic NETwork) in the United Kingdom, demonstrates how a group of librarians tried to improve the situation. Currently run by volunteers, this online information service for academic and research libraries and their users became operational in July 1991 and has already experienced astronomical growth in use. Nicholson looks at the past, present, and future of BUBL and at its relationship to other networking developments in the U.K. and elsewhere.

The success of the virtual library will depend upon the availability of fulltext resources and adequate search and retrieval mechanisms. Susan Hockey, who directs the Center for Electronic Texts in the Humanities (CETH), presents the issues involved in providing access to electronic text files. Electronic text is dynamic, not just a book in computer-readable format. The goal is to make every word searchable, so proper encoding is necessary. In addition, there must be commonly acceptable methods of documenting, cataloging, and maintaining the text files. Preservation, standardization, and international copyright issues need to be addressed in order for libraries to incorporate this medium. If primary access is through the Internet, then it is important to provide online searching and downloading functions with appropriate security. As with any new format, educational programs and support services will be required for users.

The virtual library will enable scholars to have access to original source materials in digital form and will also support an expanding market for network-based electronic journals and other publications. Michael Strangelove, an entrepreneur in this realm, was one of the original editors who tracked the evolution of electronic publications through the *Directory of Electronic Journals and Newsletters*, which is available in electronic and print formats and updated annually. Strangelove provides his philosophy and vision in the final chapter.

Laverna M. Saunders, editor

The Evolving Virtual Library: An Overview

Laverna M. Saunders
Dean of the Library and Instructional
and Learning Support
Salem State College, Salem, Massachusetts

Maurice Mitchell
Assistant Director, Internetworking
Services and Planning
System Computing Services
University and Community College System of
Nevada, Las Vegas, Nevada

"A new paradigm for conceiving and offering library services and re-sources . . . calls upon information technology to make information re-sources and services available without regard to clocks or walls . . . with powerful tools and hospitable environments for locating and communi-cating ideas and findings." (Paul Evan Peters, 12)

A process of transformation has begun. Libraries have long served as repositories of information stored in many formats, with an empha-sis on local ownership. Due to changing technology, decreasing ac-

1

quisitions budgets, the availability of electronic resources, and increasing user expectations, libraries have begun to restructure services and collections with a focus on access. Libraries using the Internet to offer or obtain bibliographic and full-text information initiated the change process. Next, information entrepreneurs created new resources and discovery tools to serve the rapidly growing population of Internet users. The potential of this information system has been described in visionary language, and the controlling image for this new era is the virtual library.

As an information system, the virtual library includes at least three dimensions: infrastructure, resources and applications, and influencing environmental forces. It is difficult to track the evolution of the virtual library due to the rapid growth and constant change of these three arenas. In the past five years, the Internet has emerged as the primary infrastructure. Subsequently, there has been a phenomenal explosion in Internet applications and resources for the end-user. As one example, the emphasis in the early 1990s was on searching library online catalogs using the telnet function. At the mid-decade point, the development of World Wide Web resources has eclipsed previous applications. The growing potential for commercial use of the Internet also influenced the political and user environment. Beginning with the assumption that the virtual library is a moving target, this review will focus on major trends with examples of landmark innovative projects which advanced the evolution of the virtual library.

Definitions

With the emergence of the virtual library, many information professionals have been forced to adopt a new lexicon. Terms have come from the disciplines of library and information science, computer science, and digital communications. Those individuals who have been deeply involved in the development of the concept of the virtual library have a general understanding of the terms associated with it. However, each of the constituents brings his/her own lexicon to the table. The librarians use strange terms such as electronic journal and postindustrial, knowledge-based society while the computer/telecommunications people use cryptic terms like TCP/IP and client-server.

The term "virtual library" gained popularity around 1990 in reports about the formation of the Coalition for Networked Information (CNI). CNI was sponsored by the Association of Research Libraries (ARL), CAUSE (the organization for the management of information technology in higher education) and EDUCOM (a consortium of colleges and universities to facilitate information technology use in higher education). Through the structure of CNI, librarians, educators, information technology professionals, government agencies, and vendors began working together to "promote the provision of information resources through existing networks and proposed interconnected networks." One of the early goals of the coalition was to "put a 'virtual library' into scholars' hands, giving them access to all information available electronically" (Turner).

The term "virtual library" comes from two related computer concepts. First, "virtual" is a way of describing a logical connection between two computer networks so that it appears transparent to a user. Second, virtual memory is a system in which the processing workspace is held partly in high-speed memory and partly on some slower and cheaper backup storage device. When the process refers to a memory location, the system hardware detects whether the required location is physically present in memory and indicates if it is not. By analogy, a "virtual library" is a system by which a user may connect transparently to remote libraries and databases using the local library's online catalog or a university or network computer as a gateway (Saunders, 1992, p. 66). Eventually, a user will be able to enter a query, get a cup of coffee, and let the computer check all the databases on the network to retrieve an answer (Turner). This scenario assumes, of course, that the necessary information—whether bibliographic, journal citation, or full text—is stored in a computer somewhere in digital format.

The virtual library can also be explained as a metaphor for the networked library, consisting of both local and remote resources, in print, electronic, and multimedia formats. In their article titled "The Network Is the Library," Kibbey and Evans elaborated on the concept that "the ideal electronic library is a range of services and collections made accessible through networks that reach beyond individual campuses or research libraries" (Kibbey and Evans, p. 16). The most comprehensive definition for the virtual library is that provided by D. Kaye Gapen:

> The virtual library has been defined as the concept of remote access to the contents and services of libraries and other information resources, combining an on-site collection of current and heavily used materials in both print and electronic form, with an electronic network which provides access to, and delivery from, external worldwide library and commercial information and knowledge sources. In essence the user is provided the effect of a library which is a synergy created by bringing together technologically the resources of many, many libraries and information services (Gapen p. 1).

Trends

In the beginning librarians learned to use the Internet by focusing on electronic mail and discussion lists. Now access to those features is so much a part of the work routine that professional conferences must provide an Internet room so attendees can keep up with the volume of mail that they receive. Use of the Internet by librarians for library functions has continued to expand. The following trends indicate how library systems and services have changed with the advent of the Internet.

Evolving library online catalogs. The Internet has provided the infrastructure for the development of a global library. In 1992, the *Internet-Accessible Library Catalogs and Databases,* compiled by Art St. George and Ron Larsen, listed a total of ninety-two U.S. libraries and 107 non-U.S. libraries. After the United States, the predominant country was the United Kingdom with seventy-two libraries, followed by Australia with nineteen. A spring 1995 search of HYTELNET produced a list of thirty-nine countries outside the U.S. which provide Internet access to their libraries. The grand total of these libraries now is 343, with the greatest numbers in the U.K. (ninety-five), Canada (seventy-two), and Australia (forty-four).

The number and types of U.S. libraries on the Internet have likewise increased dramatically. HYTELNET now lists 677 U.S. libraries and consortia. This group includes special, public, academic, and K-12 libraries and quite a list of networks. Just three years ago, the St. George-Larsen list covered ninety-two academic libraries and no public or K-12 libraries. The expansion of Internet use and access into all types of libraries is obvious, with the greatest growth yet to come in public and K-12 libraries (Saunders, 1995, p. 46).

Library online catalogs have changed to include gateways to Internet-accessible catalogs which supplement local bibliographic information. Integrated system vendors have incorporated Windows and other graphical user interfaces to make information systems easier to navigate (Rogers, 1995, pp. 27–28). Internet connectivity is transparent to the user because telnet addresses are programmed into the telecommunications software. The latest versions of integrated library systems include these features, and local online catalogs have become more sophisticated to provide Windows interfaces and Internet connectivity. Vinod Chachra, president of VTLS, Inc., describes the online catalog terminal as an "information appliance," which "as a multimedia workstation—using Z39.50 and other networking protocols—can search for a subject on the network and access indices or online catalogs that can point the searcher to digitized databases located all over the world" (VTLS). The Z39.50 protocol and client-server architecture are standard features in the latest generation of library information systems.

Digital libraries. When users had bibliographic information available online, they soon wanted full text online also. It wasn't enough to know that a book was owned by a certain library if the traditional interlibrary loan process was still required to borrow the physical item. One key trend in the evolution of the virtual library is progress toward full-text electronic resources. Recognizing the need to satisfy the electronic patron, many libraries and centers began creating full-text digital libraries. With the appropriate connectivity and software, any organization or individual can become an Internet publisher. The following projects have been selected, however, as some of the early and more serious ventures into the digital library realm.

Focusing on the "great books," Project Gutenberg (gopher:// gopher.msen.com:70/11/stuff/gutenberg) has the ambitious goal of scanning 10,000 volumes by the year 2001. The Library of International Relations is a project at the Chicago-Kent College of Law Library in which public domain United Nations documents are scanned and made available via fax (Cage). The Online Book Initiative (obi@world.std.com), based at Software Tool and Die, seeks to archive all online materials such as books, journals, catalogs, conference proceedings, technical documentation, reference works, etc. Notable among many scientific projects is the Virtual Chimps project at the University of Southern California where the papers of Jane Goodall are being digitized. In the Museum Infomatics project, staff at the University of California, Berkeley, are digitizing a valuable but brittle collection of leaves and linking description information with hypertext (Watkins). Electronic text centers which specialize in literary texts have been established at the University of Virginia (etext@virginia.edu) and at Indiana University (LETRS@indiana.edu). De Montfort University (U.K.) is also conducting a pilot project with document imaging and retrieval and classes using electronic reserve materials (Collier).

In an effort to encourage and promote research and development of electronic resources, the National Science Foundation awarded $24.4 million to six institutions: Carnegie Mellon University; the University of California, Berkeley; the University of Michigan; the University of Illinois; the University of California, Santa Barbara; and Stanford University. Begun in 1994, and scheduled to run four years, the project's focus is "to dramatically advance the means to collect, store and organize information in digital forms, and make it available for searching, retrieval, and processing via communication networks—all in user-friendly ways" (NSF PR 94-52).

Gopher sites and resources. Another trend, which complements that of digital libraries, is for library catalogs to be just one menu option on a gopher-accessible system, with many additional information resources listed. Related to this is the need for Internet searching tools to become easier and more reliable. World Wide Web browsers such as Mosaic and Netscape present a giant leap forward in organizing and searching for resources.

The Library of Congress MARVEL system (marvel.loc.gov) is a virtual grand central station for information sources. From it, one can connect to more than 102 campus-wide information systems, any of the library OPACs listed by HYTELNET, and a myriad of other databases and documents. Another multi-faceted system is the Washington and Lee Library System (liberty.uc.wlu.edu). The AskERIC system (askeric@ericir.syr.edu) provides human-mediated custom searches of the ERIC database through e-mail and includes lesson plans and other K-12 resources (http://eric.syr.edu). One of the library gopher systems worth exploring is Infoslug at the University of California, Santa Cruz (http://www.ucsc.edu).

Electronic publishing and electronic journals. The next trend contributing to the evolution of the virtual library is the gradual expansion of electronic publishing. At this point publishers are experimenting with various pricing and delivery methods to determine what model to adopt. Full-text delivery of journal articles has evolved before monographs. EBSCO and Information Access Corporation have developed full-text databases which can be accessed via the Internet or through a local network.

The number of electronic journals available on the Internet continues to grow. Several scholarly e-journals (i.e., *EJVC—the Electronic Journal on Virtual Culture*) developed out of electronic discussion groups. As universities make electronic journals and other publications accessible through gophers, libraries must decide which titles should be stored locally and which can be retrieved by remote access. One approach is that of forming consortia, and the Minnesota MINITEX PALS system plans to eventually deliver online full text to 1,400 journals. The CIC (Committee on Institutional Cooperation), a consortium of the members of the Big Ten athletic conference and the University of Chicago, has a constantly expanding number of electronic journals available on the Internet. The CIC project is a prototype electronic journal management system which "aims to be an authoritative source of electronic research and academic serial publications—incorporating all freely distributed scholarly electronic journals available online" (http://www.cic.net/cic/cic.html).

The Association of Research Libraries has tracked the growth of electronic publications and published annual editions of the *Directory of Electronic Journals, Newsletters, and Academic Discussion Lists.* The 5th Edition (1995) contains entries for nearly 2,500 scholarly lists and 675 electronic journals, newsletters, and related titles such as newsletter-digests. These figures represent an increase in size of over forty percent since the previous edition in 1994, and a 450% increase since the first edition of July 1991 (Association of Research Libraries).

Several of the science and technology publishers have collaborated with major universities to produce full-text electronic resources. One notable project is the Chemistry Online Retrieval Experiment (CORE) at Cornell University in which twenty American Chemical Society (ACS) journals, complete with illustrations, can be searched and retrieved on office computers. Carnegie Mellon University, IEEE, and Elsevier have been working on Project Mercury, scanning selected articles in computer science, artificial intelligence, and electrical and electronics engineering. The purpose of such projects is to understand how scholars use electronic tools to access large electronic collections, to evaluate several search systems, and to understand the requirements for campus storage and delivery.

Document delivery. From the growth in document delivery services provided by the various periodicals vendors (EBSCO, Faxon, Blackwell, UMI) and others (CARL, RightPages, FirstSearch), it appears that libraries are giving up local ownership and thereby control of numerous journal subscriptions. Libraries are examining their materials budgets and determining creative ways to meet user needs. This attitudinal change is important to the concept of the virtual library as an interdependent, networked system.

Integration of Internet resources. The final trend is the integration of the Internet's resources and services into basic library functions. A number of publishers and book distributors (Meckler, Addison-Wesley) have their catalogs available and provide electronic order over the Internet. Yankee Book Peddler, as one example, allows libraries to view and claim approval titles with their Folio system. Blackwell North America and B. H. Blackwell, Ltd. provide Internet searching and electronic order for more than 200,000 American and British titles. In addition to searching library catalogs over the Internet, catalogers can obtain accounts to search all of the bibliographic utilities. Downloading MARC records into the local system is still the missing link, however.

On the public services side, librarians are actively training patrons on how to search Internet resources. Pathfinders for more than seventy topics are available in the Clearinghouse of Subject-Oriented Internet Resource Guides in the University of Michigan server (http://www.lib.umich.edu/chhome. html). Scott Yanoff's subject list of Internet resources is updated regularly and is another reliable library source (http://www.uwm.edu/Mirror/inet.services.html).

Internet resources have become a standard option for reference services (Tenopir, p. 39). The traditional paper indexes have been joined by CD-ROM, tape-loaded databases available through the online public access catalog (OPAC), and now the Internet. Reference librarians face the challenge of mastering search techniques and identifying the best place to find reliable information quickly. As a strategy for assisting librarians in locating resources on the Internet, OCLC has initiated a project to catalog Internet files. Participating libraries will create, implement, test, and evaluate a searchable database of USMARC format bibliographic records, complete with electronic location and access information (USMARC field 856). The records created will be made available through the OCLC PRISM service and the FirstSearch service's WorldCat database (OCLC) (http://www.oclc.org).

Multimedia integration. With gateways linking integrated library systems, local area networks, and the Internet, libraries have the potential to combine many separate components into a complete virtual library. The Georgetown University Medical Center, for example, is developing a virtual medical library system that incorporates direct access to CD-ROM systems, document delivery, electronic journals, medical images, abstracts, bibliographic indexes, and other information services. The goal of this system is to supply its users multiple interface opportunities with medical systems (Broering).

End-user empowerment. With the evolution of the Internet as the primary infrastructure for the virtual library, programmers have developed new tools to help users search for information quickly and conveniently. Early navigational aids required the user to master computer commands. As the population of Internet users expanded beyond its academic origins, the demand grew for more user-friendly and effective searching mechanisms. Archie, developed at McGill University in Canada, is a service which scans the contents of anonymous ftp (file transfer protocol) sites around the world (Kehoe, p. 25). WAIS (Wide Area Information System) is an information retrieval tool developed by Thinking Machines Inc. WAIS provides a simple-to-use interface which allows a patron to search multiple sources of information with a single natural language question. Veronica, developed at the University of Nevada, Reno, is a service similar to Archie. While Archie searches ftp sites for files, Veronica searches all gopher sites for menu items (files, directories, and other resources) (Krol, p. 515). The World Wide Web (WWW), designed by CERN's text processing expert Tim Berners-Lee, is a hypertext system with a network of accessible information that contains billions of bytes of text and graphic elements such as drawings, photographs and diagrams (Hayes). The Web functions through a computer server. WWW browsers, such as Mosaic and Netscape, activate the hierarchical search for the Web's contents which is controlled by the Hypertext Transport Protocol (http). Taken separately or together, these powerful tools help users sift through the almost incomprehensible amount of information available on the Internet's virtual library.

Challenges remaining. The virtual library is still in its infancy, and librarians have many opportunities to contribute to its development and maturation. First, the Internet is still described as anarchy. A search by gopher, WAIS, or World Wide Web indicates that there are many "errors" and blind references to resources supposedly available on servers. There are redundant files at many sites. Some redundancy is needed in case a host is unavailable. Other times the blind alleys create garbage dumps.

Time is needed to search the Internet, and one is dependant upon all critical systems being up and responsive. Some librarians have experimented and compared the time for an Internet search and a traditional paper search. The gap can be closed if gophers are marked with "bookmarks" and librarians are familiar with the territory.

Administrators have been known to use the concept of the virtual library to make the case for budget cuts. For the foreseeable future, print resources in the form of a core collection will continue to be vital. The cost of providing online connectivity for resources such as OCLC's FirstSearch must be compared with the costs of having offline CD-ROM indexes and continuing subscriptions to paper indexes. Some users are naive enough to believe that information found only on the Internet is adequate for a literature search. Resources on the Internet can be valuable and timely if the host institution maintains the files. While there is a growing universe of information available through the Internet, libraries still need print for often-used titles. Libraries also need to provide supporting hardware for printing, downloading, and networking. The benefit of the virtual library is increased access, not reduced costs.

The increasing sophistication of library systems and access possibilities has also presented a greater need for user training. Electronic or wired classrooms are needed for teaching users to conduct Internet searches (Tenopir, p. 40). Local area networks connecting CD-ROM indexes may also be part of the total system offered to users. Librarians have had to add technical expertise and critical thinking skills to their list of learning outcomes.

Finally, the virtual library is dependent upon the infrastructure of the Internet. Governance of the Internet is political, and library interests and needs must be represented as federal policies evolve. Access, especially for public libraries and K-12, must be protected as commercial and private use grows.

State Library Networks

Building the infrastructure for the virtual library has been costly. In order to obtain computer hardware and cabling, librarians and computer specialists have collaborated. They have created the necessary networks and operating agreements to establish and maintain networks within geographical areas. Statewide library networks have largely been the result of grants from the federal government (such as the Department of Education's Title II-D program and the Department of Commerce's Telecommunications and Information Infrastructure Assistance Program), philanthropic foundations, and even some realignment of budgetary priorities at the local level. Nearly every state has received grant funding. Some of the pioneer networks are described here.

CARL (Colorado Alliance of Research Libraries), best known of the state library networks, was formed in the mid-1970s so that six libraries could share resources. It has grown to include more than thirty libraries, both public and academic, in several western states. The CARL system, the technical components of CARL, has been installed in nine different locales, ranging from Hawaii to the East coast of the U.S. (Lenzini, 1991).

OhioLink grew out of a 1987 study on the future of libraries which was conducted for the Ohio Board of Regents. Instead of new buildings, the study recommended that the board create a statewide electronic catalog system and high density remote storage facilities. OhioLink's goal is "to give public and private colleges and universities, municipalities, and private organizations easy access to printed and electronic materials in the state's principal academic libraries" ("On-Line," 1991).

NEON (Nevada Education Online Network) is an initiative of the academic libraries of the University and Community College System of Nevada and the UCCSN System Computing Services. Funded in part through a grant from the Department of Education, the project has created a statewide network so that patrons in any of the participating libraries have ubiquitous access to the OPACs and databases throughout the system as well as access to many resources found on the Internet. Future extentions of NEON include interconnection with the public library systems in the state as well as interconnectivity with the K-12 community.

K-12 Networks

The Internet, and the virtual library, has had particular influence on the K-12 environment over the past several years. Thousands of teachers across the U.S. have discovered resources such as databases, libraries, lesson plan collections, and colleagues with similar concerns and teaching ideas. There has been phenomenal growth in both the numbers of K-12 educators with access and the number and quality of connected resources for education. Several of the pioneers in providing access for K-12 educators were the Texas Education Network (TENET) (see following chapter by Stout); VAPEN (the Virginia Public Education Network); and Florida's Information Resource Network (FIRN). In 1992, FIRNMAIL, a part of FIRN, provided services to more than 6,000 public educators (Florida Department of Education). In the past few years, Internet use in K-12 has exploded, and millions of K-12 students now use the Internet as a virtual library and laboratory. Examples of current K-12 applications include a hotlist of K-12 Internet school sites (http://toons.cc.ndsu.nodak.edu/~sackmann/k12.html) and Kids Web (http://www.npac.syr.edu/textbook/kidsweb/).

There are at least two disadvantages linked with the virtual library and K-12 education that come immediately to mind: misperception caused by the medium and "technology equity" such as access. The first instance is illustrated by a situation that occured when a group of elementary children in Las Vegas, Nevada, invited an "electronic pen pal" to a school party. The young people couldn't handle the geography—the fact that the pen pal was in Oklahoma, yet their communication was nearly real time. The students felt that the pen pal "just had to be here in Las Vegas."

Today, the biggest problem with the virtual library is that those who have access enjoy the advantages. Access is relatively expensive and crosses several political jurisdictions. First, a teacher or student needs a computer or terminal, then a connection to an Internet host. Getting a line into a school in many U.S. locations often takes a minimum of six months and crosses at least three turfdoms. These challenges do not take into account the initial and on-going telecommunications costs. There is another side of the equity problem: the poor school with no parent-teacher organization and a skeptical principal.

The solution for K-12 Internet connectivity is "developing communities of teachers and learners" (Clement, p. 22). Enabling access to people and resources as well as the development of community-building projects and supportive infrastructure is key. The challenges are to make sure that every part of K-12 education is involved in the process, to work toward the goal of widespread connectivity, and to achieve a connected "critical mass" of K-12 educators.

A number of notable K-12 projects have developed over the past few years. Many of these projects have included experiments to examine how the curriculum and practicum could be changed locally to take advantage of the technology (Clement, p. 22). The Chamber of Commerce's Community Learning and Information Network sought to put into schools computers and interactive video linked by local area networks which were linked by two-way satellite transmissions. The Office of Education Research and Improvement in the U.S. Department of Education, in its SMARTLINE project, made the information resources of the department available on the Internet. The America 2000 effort called for telecommunications linkages between one or more schools in every Congressional district in the country (Clement, p. 20). The California Technology Project upgraded its platform and interface and worked with Pacific Bell to provide local-call telecommunications connections and Internet access to every educator in the state, through the Knowledge Network project. The Consortium for School Networking (CoSN) was created to provide a leadership mechanism and a forum so that K-12 educators could develop both policies and practices in order to make use of telecommunications that advance educational reform (gopher digital.cosn.org; http://www.cosn.org/).

The virtual library, as we currently know it, is an out-growth of the research community with tools created by scientists and programmers. In the 1960s, when computers were first introduced in substantial scale to the nation's schools, no one dreamed that anyone would ever use computers as communications and access tools. In the 1970s only an enterprising high school teacher realized that computers could be used for personal productivity like word processing instead of CAI (computer assisted instruction/ programmed instruction). It would be a mistake to expect that the K-12 community will simply do more of the same kind of things that we characterize as the virtual library. K-12 teachers have demonstrated amazing innovation when they begin to use a technology somebody else developed. The safest prediction here is that K-12 teachers and students will make some sort of neat, dramatic, and fully unexpected left turn in the "future roles" course.

Impact on Instruction

In 1990 we proposed an agenda for the decade which acknowledged that instruction would change with the advent of the virtual library (Mitchell and Saunders). At the mid-decade point, the weekly "Information Technology" section of *The Chronicle of Higher Education* features issues and case studies of Internet applications in colleges and universities (i.e., DeLoughry). The term "virtual college" has been adopted to refer to degree courses and programs which are offered remotely through interactive networked technologies (Jacobson, p. A21). An exploration of the Internet on any subject will yield a list of outlines, current or obsolete, of courses offered at universities all over the world.

Most institutions of higher education now offer e-mail accounts to students and faculty. Within K-12 schools, select classes may obtain access through a local university or the community network. Student and faculty dependence upon the Internet has grown to such an extent that colleges and universities are exploring how best to offer access beyond the local dial-up radius of campus (Wilson, p. A20).

The reliance of obtaining information through computers has influenced California State University administrators to eliminate a physical library in their planning for a new campus in the Monterey Bay. Even dormitories are being wired for students to have voice and data lines at their desktop, and some schools require students to supply their own PC (Hafner, p. 62–3).

We still anticipate that the virtual library will have a significant effect on the teaching-learning process. However, we still have some issues to resolve before capability will become acceptability, not the least of which is the general acceptance of technological solutions. Children who have computers in their homes learn early to use them for school assignments. Teachers and external organizations such as those which sponsor contests may undermine a child's enthusiasm and initiative by requiring papers to be submitted in ink. Some real issues that must be addressed include: electronic signatures (verification of authorship); technology equity (access to the virtual library is necessary before students can use it); and the big one, teachers (who can help or hinder the use of the virtual library).

For the indoctrinated, the virtual library is relatively easy and convenient to use. Research can be accomplished much more easily than by the old-fashioned way, submerged in a pile of reference books and trays from the card catalog and the resulting stack of three-by five-inch cards. How then, can the teacher be sure that the student actually did the work? We're still saddled by some old verification problems. We are still some time away from an electronic signaturing technology that will put the issue aside.

Those of us in "connected" institutions take the virtual library for granted. Based on a Wide Area Network (WAN) concept, the virtual library is still only an idea for many. Even at this mid-decade point it is clear that not every school or college in the United States is able to participate. According to Robert C. Heterick (1993), President of EDUCOM, in a testimony before Congress directed toward the NREN initiative, "Only half of the U. S. four-year institutions are linked today, and fewer than that for two-year institutions." No reliable information is currently available about the extent of K-12 connectivity to the Internet. Heterick went on to state, "More libraries need to be connected along with high schools and state agencies." Whatever the case, it is apparent that many, many students and teachers don't have access. Under such conditions, any dramatic impact on the teaching-learning process is diffused.

Teachers can help or hinder the use of the virtual library. Issues of access and verification of authorship aside, teachers are still in the driver's seat when it comes to any real impact on instruction. Teachers who encourage use of the electronic world, whether for e-mail or for locating and retrieving information from the "virtual library," will insure a positive impact. Teachers who penalize their students for employing information technology, however that ocurrs, will hinder the use of the virtual library. At present, a few students learn about the virtual library in informal ways. Most students still learn about the virtual library from a librarian or a teacher who champions the use of digital telecommunications.

Scenario for the Future

The next generation of OPACs will be virtual—they'll 'exist' only during a particular use and they won't look the same to any two users. Instead, an ever expanding collection of information servers (computers handling local databases) will be linked by networks to provide the user with the comforting illusion of a single system.

Most activity on this system will be initiated outside the library's walls. Freed at last from meetings about where terminals should be placed and endless debates over the efficacy of help screen text, library systems staff will instead fret over whether sufficient local node resources are available to support the drop-in user and his pocket interface unit. There may still be a few terminals for public use, but they'll be like the library's newspaper—there for the few folks who either didn't buy one or forgot to bring it with them to the library. Your computer will sign on to this OPAC.

Users will determine the interface. Vendors will offer a variety of personal information management packages for these little computers and most users will use a personally designed/customized interface. Queries, created on the personal unit will be uploaded to the library's local processor, parsed apart and sent to various remote hosts. Responses will be collated, and either immediately (or at some later time—depending on how many people are still using NREN to write long messages like this) relayed back to the pocket unit. . . . The results of this OPAC session will be transferred to the home or office workstation for subsequent work. (Grotophorst)

In 1992 Grotophorst suggested that "we're probably still a generation away from this sort of system (which would require a more robust networking environment than the Internet provides, and a marketplace that adheres to at least some minimum interoperability standards)." Just a few years later, the "over the counter" technology was at the threshold of providing just such capability! The advent of Mosaic, expansion of WAIS technology, the availability of personal digital assistants (PDAs) such as Apple's Newton and wireless communications position us to do queries such as suggested above. The notable difference now is that the intervention of the library host is now unnecessary.

Here is another twist for the future: In the global information system, every computer becomes both a client and a server. The distinction of OPAC vs. scholar's workstation vs. database server vs. personal computer becomes blurred. In a far-reaching scenario, any personal workstation can store information for use by someone other than the host's owner, thus acting as a server. Among other implications, this means the the PC must be left on around the clock so that clients such as gopher and Mosaic can make connections. Such behavior drastically changes our perception of the personal workstation. Yes, it is still *our* personal tool . . . but it is also someone else's! At this point, we will have moved to the other end of the continuum—from many terminals connecting to a few hosts/servers to only hosts (all computers) connecting to each other. The virtual library, with all sorts of information sources dropping in and out of the network, may be defined as a truly dynamic information system.

References

Association of Research Libraries. "ARL 5th Edition of Directory of Electronic Publications Available." (18 May 1995): press release.

Broering, Naomi C. "Georgetown University: The Virtual Medical Library." *Computers in Libraries* 13, no. 2 (Feb. 1993): 13.

Cage, Mary Crystal. "The Virtual Library." *The Chronicle of Higher Education* 41, no. 4 (21 Sept. 1994): A23.

Clement, John. "Where We Are in Networking for K-12 Education: A First Annual Review."· *EDUCOM Review* 27, no. 5 (Sept./Oct. 1992): 20–23.

Collier, Mel W., Anne Ramsden, and Zimin Wu. "The Electronic Library: Virtually a Reality?" Pp. 136–146 in *Opportunity 2000: Understanding and Serving Users in an Electronic Library*, ed. by Ahmed H. Helal and Joachim W. Weiss. Universitatsbibliothek Essen: Essen, 1993.

DeLoughry, Thomas J. "Will Higher Education Thrive or Wither in Cyberspace?" *The Chronicle of Higher Education* (27 Jan. 1995): A22.

Duderstadt, James J. "An Information Highway to the Future." *EDUCOM Review* 27, no. 5 (Sept./Oct. 1992): 36–41.

Florida Department of Education. *The FIRN Report.* Tallahassee, FL, December, 1992.

Gapen, D. Kaye. "The Virtual Library: Knowledge, Society and the Librarian." Pp 1–14 in *The Virtual Library: Visions and Realities*, ed. by Laverna M. Saunders. Westport, Conn.: Meckler, 1993.

Grotophorst, Clyde W. "Re: OPAC Functionality," 17 June 1992, online posting, PACS-L discussion list (PACS-L@UHUPVM1.BITNET).

Hafner, Katie. "Wiring the Ivory Tower." *Newsweek* (30 Jan. 1995): 62–66.

Hayes, Brian. "The World Wide Web." *American Scientist* 82, no. 5 (Sept./Oct. 1994): 416–421.

Jacobson, Robert L. "The 'Virtual College'." *The Chronicle of Higher Education* (27 Jan. 1995): A21.

Kehoe, Brendan P. *Zen and the Art of the Internet: A Beginner's Guide to the Internet*, 1st Ed. January, 1992.

Kibbey, Mark and Nancy H. Evans. "The Network Is the Library." *Educom Review* (Fall 1989): 16.

Krol, Ed. *The Whole Internet: User's Guide & Catalog*, 2nd ed. Sebastopol, CA: O'Reilly & Associates, Inc., 1994.

Lenzini, Rebecca T. "Reactions From an Automation Vendor." In *The Evolution of Library Automation: Management Issues and Future Perspectives*, ed. by Gary M. Pitkin. Westport, Conn.: Meckler, 1991.

Marine, A. (Ed.). *Internet: Getting Started.* Menlo Park, CA: SRI International, 1992.

Mitchell, Maurice and Laverna M. Saunders. "The Virtual Library: An Agenda for the 1990s." *Computers in Libraries* 11, no. 4 (April 1991): 8–11.

NSF PR 94-52. "NSF Announces Awards for Digital Libraries Research." (URL: http://www.nsf.gov/).

OCLC. "OCLC Seeks Participants in Internet Cataloging Project." (3 Mar. 1995): press release.

"On Line." *Chronicle of Higher Education* (6 Nov. 1991): A24.

Peters, Paul Evan. "Thinking in Terms of Enterprise-Wide Opportunities and Challenges." *EDUCOM Review* 27, no. 6 (November/Dec. 1992): 12–14.

Rogers, Michael. "Preservation Community & Research Libs. Form Digital Library Fed." *Library Journal* 120, no. 11 (15 June 1995): 23.

Rogers, Michael. "Windows and Internet Access Offer Big Push at ALA Midwinter." *Library Journal* 120, no. 5 (15 Mar. 1995): 27–28.

Saunders, Laverna. "From the Editor." *Computers in Libraries* 15, no. 2 (Feb. 1995): 46.

Saunders, Laverna M. "The Virtual Library Today." *Library Administration and Management* 6, no. 2 (Spring 1992): 66–70.

St. Lifer, Evan and Michael Rogers. "Many Libraries Find Their Walls Are Tumbling Down." *Library Journal* 120, no. 6 (1 Apr. 1995): 14.

Tenopir, Carol. "Integrating Electronic Reference." *Library Journal* 120, no. 6 (1 Apr. 1995): 39–40.

Turner, Judith A. "Coalition Plans to Organize Information on Computer Networks. *The Chronicle of Higher Education*: (21 Mar. 1990): A20.

VTLS News Release. "VTLS Inc., Library of Virginia Sponsor Virtual Library Seminars." 12 Sept. 1994.

Watkins, Beverly T. "Computerized Catalogs Extend Access to Specialized Collections." *The Chronicle of Higher Education* 38, no. 40 (10 June 1992): A15–17.

Wilson, David L. "Internet@home." *The Chronicle of Higher Education* (16 June 1995): A20–25.

Linking K-12 Educators in Texas: Texas Education Network

Connie Stout
Director, Texas Education Network
Austin, Texas

T exas is a diverse state with more than 1,050 school districts that range in size from student populations of more than 190,000 to fewer than ten. More than 3.2 million students and over 200,000 teachers, support staff, and administrators work in Texas schools each day. The Texas Education Agency has long recognized the need for effective and low-cost communication among and between the more than 6,400 public school campuses, the twenty regional education service centers, colleges, and universities, and other educational professionals. In 1985, the agency had contracted for an electronic network with THE ELECTRIC PAGES, a commercial network operated by GTE (a major phone company). The TEA-NET (Texas Education Agency Network) had also provided e-mail and bulletin boards to approximately 650 of the administrative offices in the school district. Legislative mandate required the state board of education to present a plan for technology. In 1987, Dr. William Kirby, commissioner of education, appointed an advisory committee to assess the needs of the state and to develop a strategic plan for the use of technology. In November of 1988, the state board of education adopted the 1988–2000 Long-Range Plan for Technology. Incorporated within the plan was a request to establish a K-12 statewide communications network to link all school districts and their campuses. The requests were incorporated into Senate Bill 650, which was passed by the 71st Legislature. Senate Bill 650 (Section 14.042 of the Texas Education Code) authorized the establishment and maintenance of an electronic information transfer system, the Texas Education Network (TENET).

The agency evaluated alternatives for the acquisition of services necessary for the creation and maintenance of an enhanced electronic communications network capable of transmitting information among and between the members of the public education system in Texas. Teachers, administrators, the regional service centers, and the educational organizations that had been utilizing the TEA-NET network within the state were surveyed for their input into what was desired in a telecomputing network. In addition, a nationwide review of telecomputing networks and telecomputing hardware, software, and training was conducted. The telecomputing networks reviewed included proprietary networks such as GTE's Special Net, CompuServe, AT&T, AppleLink, America Online and statewide networks such as Pennsylvania's PennLink, Florida's FIRN, Virginia's VAPEN; and other grassroots networks like People Sharing Information Network (PSInet), FrEdMail, and the Fidonet news-groups K12-net. It was apparent that a number of barriers existed that prevented the integration of telecomputing networks into K-12 education. In order to achieve successful implementation of an educational network, strategies to address these barriers had to be employed.

Barriers to K-12 Networks

Lack of Access

Telecomputing requires access to phone lines, computers, modems, and local area networks connected to a wide area network. A recent survey of Texas revealed that there were more than 84,000 phone jacks in the 1,058 school districts. However, only two percent of the classrooms had access to a phone line. In addition, telephones were in limited quantity in campus administrative offices. In one district, parent volunteers who came to the school to contact absent students brought their own cellular phones because the office phones were limited or unavailable. To add to this burden, school districts are required to pay the same rates as businesses for a phone line. These rates vary with phone companies and range between $11.25 to $55 per month. With an average of forty faculty in a building, this was seen as an overwhelming barrier.

Only within the last few years have sufficient numbers of computers reached a large number of teachers. Network models initially found in schools were usually proprietary district-wide or were school-wide administrative and management-oriented systems which didn't allow communication and access to resources by teachers and students. The first computers in the classroom, usually found in the computer science, mathematics, or business education classrooms, were the focus of instruction. As a rule, these computers were not linked with a local area network and instructional telecomputing was limited to individual modem connections. Where there was an installed base of networked computers in schools, one usually did not find models that showed connections to a wide area network. The model of one phone line, one modem, and one computer was not a model that would scale considering the large numbers of potential educators and students involved in the educational system.

Multiple Protocols

Unlike the university community in which the Internet has arisen as a primary standard, the members of the K-12 education community witnessed the development of numerous electronic networks. While the Internet developed as a network of networks, most telecomputing technology in K-12 education was based upon individual computers dialing a central host. These networks were not compatible and had diverse protocol standards. As a result, a critical mass of users could not be achieved on any one network. Educators could not communicate with one another unless they were on the same network, and the diverse numbers seemed to inhibit the growth of any one system. The industry seemed to be unstable, and networks such as MIX (McGraw Hill Information Exchange), the SOURCE, and the ELECTRIC PAGES were unable to survive.

In addition, many of these networks supported a specific computer hardware. Schools that adopted one standard (such as Apple) of computer hardware were unwilling to purchase another standard (such as IBM compatibles) just to access the computer network. This was further complicated by telecommunications protocols and software. Whereas there are different telephone instruments, it makes no difference what instrument is dialed for a connection to be established, even when someone is in another state using another instrument and another telephone company. This type of interoperability was not possible in K-12 telecomputing.

Cost and Price Structures

Because the rise in K-12 telecomputing technology was based upon individual computers and modems accessing a network over telephone lines, the metered rate for online services was identified as another major obstacle to the use of telecomputing technologies. Educational institutions based their budgets on fixed prices. Most K-12 educational organizations are unable to justify non-fixed rates. An "open purchase order" is not a viable option for a school district. School administrations were able to justify the use of telecomputing technologies in limited cases. Many pilot programs that flourished did so as long as grant monies for connections lasted.

Lack of Training and Support

Training on telecomputing networks was not tailored to the needs of educators and was not incorporated into their routine curriculum. Hence, there were very few incentives for educators to become involved in telecomputing. Training, where it existed, did not extend beyond a technical focus to illustrate ways to help the novice consumer understand the benefits of electronic communications as an enhancement to personal productivity or access to enriched resources for the classroom. Those who did decide to utilize the telecomputing networks did so outside training models found in the school institution. To be able to make the initial connections, educators had to purchase a modem at the local computer store, install the modem in their computer, and configure the communications software to the appropriate parity and baud rate. This was done before the first connection was made. Not only did telecomputing require an understanding of the operation of the computer and modem, it also required an understanding of word processing and file transfer. It was apparent that the hardest connection to make was the first one. Once the connection was made, there was a question about how applicable the information was that was to be incorporated into their jobs.

There was a lack of consistent ongoing support. Support for the non-technical consumer was difficult because of the number of variables. The difficulty could have been with the communications software, the computer, the modem, the phone line, or the network itself. Frequently, technical support was an ad hoc effort from other telecomputing users on the network. This informal means of support was good, but could not be seen as consistent.

Lack of an Intuitive User Interface

Another barrier to overcome with the earlier adoption was the lack of "tools" to enable the educators to send messages across the network. The communications software on the personal computer has not been seen as intuitive. Additionally, there were large numbers of communications software packages, each with different commands and terms. Many of the networks required online connections for work to be executed while the majority of educators wanted to prepare files offline and to send them when it was more convenient to their work schedule.

Lack of an Understanding of Telecomputing Benefits

The numbers of educators who had direct experience with this technology were limited to the early adopters, those who had special funding, or those with special single purpose administrative networks. This severely limited the development of an understanding of the educational value of incorporating electronic communications into daily use. Because there were a number of different networks and the cost was seen as a barrier, a void existed. These barriers inhibited administrative support to fund further study of the benefits of telecomputing technologies.

Comprehensive Approach

It was felt that a complete communications infrastructure design with a comprehensive approach was necessary to overcome the number of barriers that were apparent in K-12 education. After extensive research and collaboration with other states, it became apparent that two states, Virginia and Texas, clearly were considering a similar approach. A position paper on the areas of architecture, interface, and equity was developed through a series of meetings with principals (Bull, et al., 1989). Although similar in design, the process and implementation were somewhat different. In Texas, a Request for Proposal process was initially tried, and in November of 1991, the proposal was withdrawn. Because the process did not result in an award, alternatives were considered.

On December 9, 1991, the High-Performance Computing Act was signed into law. The act called for the development of the National Research and Education Network (NREN). This network would give rise to hope that a national education network could be established upon Internet protocols. Senator Al Gore felt this could result in school reform when he stated:

> This network could revolutionize American education as well as giving teachers new tools and new ways to inspire their students. Today hundreds of elementary and secondary schools are linked to the NSFNET, enabling students to exchange messages with other students throughout the country and enabling teachers to share new teaching ideas with one another (Gore, 1991).

With an awareness of the national networking initiative and an analysis of the available networking alternatives, it was decided that an approach based upon interagency contracts with the University of Texas System for Telecommunications services was the option that would realize both the most cost-effective system and increased services to Texas K-12 students and educators. The Texas Higher Education Network (THEnet), providing connectivity to the majority of the major post-secondary institutions in the state, is a National Science Foundation (NSF) regional network, connected to thousands of other networks worldwide through the Internet. Several other states, including California and Florida were using similar models to bring connectivity to their public school educators.

This decision was the strategy employed to overcome the barrier of multiple protocols. It resulted in the formulation of three essential requirements for the Texas network:

- Network standards that would allow this network to scale upward as growth and new advanced technology demanded.
- Network standards based upon TCP/IP (Transmission Control Protocol/Internet Protocol) and OSI (Open Systems Interconnection) protocols to permit interoperability between networking systems.
- Network standards for a Unix-based operating system to permit multi-tasking for educators using the system.

Through shared resources a critical mass of people could communicate with others across many different networks. This gave TENET the capability to have e-mail gateways to many other major networks. These networks include AppleLink, CompuServe, MCI mail, AT&T mail, FrEdMail, and Fidonet. Now educators could communicate with their colleagues across the state or nation, using the network with which they were most familiar.

The issue of access cost was minimized throughout the state when Texas established a set of annual registration fees for all educators. Individuals could dial a number, certify themselves as a full-time Texas educator, and apply for an account. No online fees were charged to the consumer, regardless of where the access was made in the state. The registration fee, established at $5 per year for Texas educators in public education, varies according to customer category, with other categories paying a larger amount.

Local access is available from seventeen major metropolitan centers in the state (see Figure 1). From these centers, seventy-five percent of the population can be reached with a local phone call. Toll-free lines are available to educators located outside the local calling areas.

Access to the technology equipment was identified as an equity issue. The Sixth Called Session of the 71st Legislature passed Senate Bill 1, which established the Technology Allotment Fund. The provisions of that legislation (Subchapter D, Section 14.061) became effective in September of 1992. The Technology Allotment Fund was initially set at $30 per average daily attendance (ADA). It is to increase by $5 per ADA each year until it reaches $50 per ADA. In addition, Senate Bill 351, Regular Session of the 72nd Legislature eliminated a separate Technology Fund and maintained the incremental increase of funding. The technology allotment is now included in Tier 1 of the Foundation School Program. The allocation is to be used for

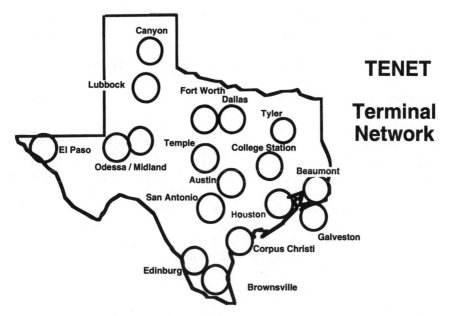

Figure 1. TENET's major metropolitan centers

the acquisition of technological equipment and related services, including hardware, software, courseware, training, subscription fees for telecommunications and database services, and other related services. To apply for the funds, schools submitted a plan for the use of technology within their districts. This strategy began to relieve other barriers of access.

The strategy used to overcome training and support issues was a multifaceted approach. Initially, the Texas Education Agency contracted with the Texas Center for Educational Technology, which worked with agency staff, teachers, and administrators to design a curriculum based on three areas: use of the network, conference moderation, and curriculum integration. Forty Texas educators, representing a broad range of expertise, were selected as TENET Master Trainers. Twenty of the trainers were from each of the educational service centers, an intermediate unit between the state department of education and the local school district. The education service centers have a relationship with local school districts and offer a broad spectrum of professional development and in-service courses for educators. The additional twenty trainers represented school librarians, math supervisors, computer coordinators, and representatives from professional organizations such as the Texas Computer Education Association (TCEA), the Texas Association of School Boards (TASB), the Texas Association for Supervision and Curriculum Development (TASCD), and the Texas State Teachers Association (TSTA).

The TENET Master Trainers offered training to facilitators in all 1,058 school districts. Copies of the training materials and the communications software, Kermit, were provided to all school districts. This training enabled district facilitators to offer the first level of support for district personnel utilizing TENET. Training is also provided through a number of the affiliate professional associations, which maintain a news and conference area on TENET.

After one year, the training was revised by a group of the Master Trainers. Three Master Trainers, incorporating revisions from their colleagues, developed a new users guide. The manual was developed online during the summer. These educators, located in different areas of the state, only met once during the summer to develop the guide. They used the network to communicate with each other and to share their thoughts. The guide was then reviewed by other Master Trainers before it was made available. It can be downloaded from the network or ordered from the University of Texas, Office of Telecommunications Services. Currently training has been incorporated into the staff development offerings of the twenty regional education service centers and the classes in institutions of higher education.

In addition to conference areas in which technical information is available online, support is also provided by the TENET help-desk. Texas educators can speak to a member of the staff of the help-desk located at the University of Texas for continued support. The personalized interaction is a vital component of the support for the network.

Network Components

The University of Texas Office of Telecommunications Services designed a menu system for TENET by which educators are offered a variety of services that they can access using their computer, modem, and communications software with VT 100 terminal emulation. The basic components of the TENET network include e-mail, news and conferencing, and access to databases. Because TENET is a subnetwork of THEnet, educators are provided with full Internet capabilities. These services include telnet, the capability that permits educators to remotely access other computers on the Internet, and remote file transfer protocol (ftp), the capability that permits sharing computer files across networks.

The first item on the menu is e-mail. For this service, TENET supports Pine 3.0, designed by the University of Washington. Pine, a menu-driven mail system, has many features that educators enjoy. These include filing mail in folders, creating mail aliases, personalizing mailing lists, importing and exporting files, supporting mime, and permitting files to be attached. The text editor, Pico, was seen to be very user-friendly.

TASS was selected as a newsreader to enable educators an easier way to manage news and conference items. Access to a wealth of resources was a first consideration of the network. The Internet has the ability to share newsfeeds throughout the many networks through USENET newsfeeds. By using this capability TENET was able to access a number of resources. A critical need of educators was the expressed ability to receive time-sensitive news. To address this need, TENET contracted with Clarinet for UPI newsfeeds. In addition, Texas educators receive news from UNnews. Other national resources available via newsfeeds are the CNN Daily Lesson plan and Newsweek guides. Resources include access to the McDonald Observatory's Stardate, NSF's Geometry Forum, the state's Parks and Wildlife Fishing Report, and a number of listserv conferences, such as KidsNet, and a listserv discussing the appropriate use of the TI graping calculator.

TENET also supports Texas-specific conferences. Some of the conferences have been established by various professional groups. This has allowed colleagues throughout the state to share common interests. However, all of the TENET conferences are moderated by educators. A conference moderator is able to create an environment for learning and a place in which network etiquette can be established. All educators functioning in the role as moderator on TENET receive training to help, nurture, and guide conference participants as they begin to explore the use of telecommunications. Conferences are established based upon request by Texas educators. These conferences are subject or area specific. In areas such as science, outcome-based assessment permits practitioners within the state to participate in direct dialogue with decision makers. This one feature enabled educators to feel the impact that technology has brought, providing them a voice in how educational policy is shaped.

Another feature on the TENET menu permits educators in Texas to have access to the resources on the Internet. Accessing the Internet has been compared to trying to take a sip of water from a fire hydrant. The menu allows a short list of what has been identified by some as the most valued resources on the Internet for educators. By selecting a menu item, TENET customers can access NASA's Spacelink at the Marshall Space Flight Center in Huntsville, Alabama, or the Underground Weather at the University of Michigan. Other resources have been added as customers and the TENET Master Trainers identify what the majority of the community would like to access.

Finding other colleagues on the network has been given priority. Teachers are able to access the Directory and locate other educators on the network. Teachers can list themselves in Directory Assistance. Educators feel it is very important to be able to locate colleagues and others who share common interests. This is illustrated by the following comment:

I teach journalism and am the ONLY person on my campus who is responsible for the yearbook, newspaper, Journalism I, photo-journalism, and other assorted details that go along with those responsibilities. Few of my fellow teachers can come close to understanding what my job is like or even help me with some of the problems I face each day. But I know that I can log onto TENET and share with my journalism friends across the state a desktop publishing trick that I learned at workshop, a place to find information on a story my students are working on, or just call to tell them about my day.

—Pat Gathright, MacArthur High School, North East ISD

The file transfer area of the TENET menu permits the practitioner to download specific files. For instance, the file that contained the form that districts needed to fill out for the Technology Allotment Fund was placed on TENET. The Lotus Spreadsheet that permitted districts to calculate the estimated state aid was also placed on the network. The TENET manual was also provided to network users in the same fashion.

An option was provided for TENET users to change their password, select a mail reader, or view their personal files stored on the network. The final option was established to permit specialized information databases. The Texas Association of School Boards has an area for legislative bill tracking. This feature has enabled districts throughout the state to understand legislation as it moves through the legislature. Other features are found in the Wide Area Information System (WAIS). Because Texas provides to its clients a site license for *Grolier's Encyclopedia,* the network is able to use a WAIS client to provide such information resources as *Grolier's,* an EPIE database of software, ERIC digest, and Project Gutenberg.

After one year some observations can be made about the development of the network. The growth has been exponential (see Figure 2). The earlier anticipated population of 3,000 was surpassed within the first three months. Since the network began operation on August 26, 1991, more than 16,000 users are accessing TENET. Eighty percent of those users are K-12 educators. Of those, the majority at this time are administrators, coordinators, or librarians. The largest population growth at this time is seen in classroom teachers. TENET is averaging 80,500 log-ins per month, and more than 1,000 new users apply for an account each month. There has been a steady increase in network usage. When the capability is available for teachers to add classroom accounts to their own account, it is anticipated that the network will experience another period of exponential growth.

Reflections on TENET

A study of network use has been revealing. Within the first few weeks more than 500 educators requested accounts on TENET. At its peak, The Electric Page served administrative offices in about 560 school districts.

Within the first three months, more customers had registered for accounts on the network than had been estimated for the first year. The jagged chart (see Figure 3) indicates that the log-in rate declined on the weekend, but did not drop completely off the chart. It was easy to recognize the first Thanksgiving holiday as teachers went home for vacation. Once the first winter holiday approached, it was anticipated that network use would drop dramatically, if not altogether. However, even on December 25, more than 500 educators logged onto TENET—most likely with their new modems or computers. An inter-

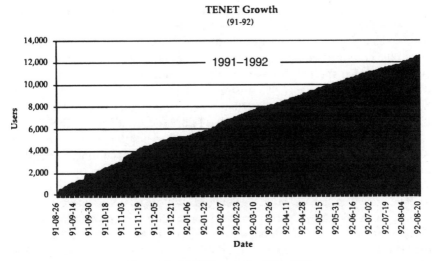

Figure 2. TENET growth, 1991-1992

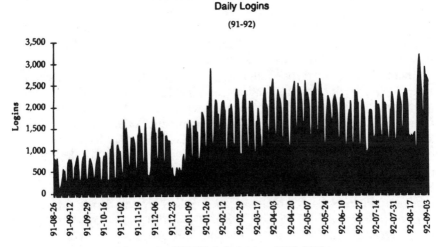

Figure 3. TENET daily logins, 1991-1992

esting peak occurred in late January when the coaches were able to receive their redistricting alignment through access to TENET. It clearly emphasized the need for timely information that could not be obtained in another fashion. After the initial first year, staff at the university were delighted with the approach of the summer holidays. They again anticipated a dramatic drop in network use; however, use of TENET was not reduced. This was the first time that many of the educators were able to spend time researching the many resources of TENET and the Internet that could be of value to their students.

The technology has enabled teachers to communicate with one another. It was interesting that a statewide network opened communications patterns not yet realized before. Teachers have been traditionally isolated from their colleagues even though they were in the same building. It was realized that electronic communications were just as important, if not more important, for educators down the hall from each other to communicate with each other over a network. As one TENET customer exclaimed, "They just don't know how hungry we are for this." Another teacher said, "I have found a revitalization in my own teaching process that I attribute to utilizing TENET."

Network demands have resulted in the need for local area networks within buildings. With more than 16,000 educational practitioners using the network, demand on network resources has resulted in busy signals. Teachers who want to use the network as a classroom tool need to be able to have access to the network on demand. With teachers wanting students to have network access, a real concern for scaling the network has arisen. Carrollton-Farmers Branch Independent School District, a school district in the Dallas/Ft. Worth metroplex, has established a local area network in each of the campuses. Teachers within that school district have a direct connection to the TENET network via a wide area network. This approach is a strategy that will overcome the burden of a dial-up system, give teachers access to a high speed, on-demand connection, and is a model that can fit the new demands of the information age. They will be able to share many district-wide resources and have access to the statewide resources.

There is also a need for local autonomy over authentication. Whereas a statewide network could authenticate certified Texas educators, there was a need to provide access to another important segment of the educational community, the parents and community members. Although parents were initially permitted access to the network, these accounts have had to be denied because of the overwhelming growth and the need for the authentication of parent accounts to be held as a local decision. Like Carrollton-Farmers Branch ISD, a number of school districts are considering direct access to TENET. Early communication pilots by the Texas Education Agency and two school districts revealed that districts enjoyed designing their own community bulletin boards and were able to have a communications system within their districts that were reflective of their community.

Community colleges, public libraries, and many other state agencies have requested access to the network. The communications infrastructure has enabled populations that have been isolated to find a common ground upon which to communicate. Several groups have initiatives in place to develop their own communications infrastructures.

Although initially funded to support administrative communications between the central education agency and the school districts, the network has been able to link both administrative and instructional communities. Certification officers in the education service centers can communicate directly to authenticate teachers' records, and universities and school districts are piloting the transfer of student transcripts. It is the extension of these benefits to the classroom that has been most enlightening.

Here are a few of the comments made by educators about TENET's value:

In a large majority of the districts in Texas, there are limited resources due to the small size of the communities and/or the remoteness. TENET is a means of providing a step toward equity of resources to our districts, allowing the teacher to truly "bring the world to class."

—*Raylene Renfrow, Master Trainer, Region VI, Education Service Center*

This year we are involved in several projects. About twenty scientists have agreed to communicate with my students and answer their questions via e-mail. This has been very successful; you can literally see the students' self-esteem and interest in science expand when they receive a personal reply to their question from a scientist.

—*Kirk Beckendorf, Fredricksburg Middle School, Fredricksburg ISD*

Telecommunications projects are an ongoing part of development for many Texas educators. One such project is an example of how telecommunications can bring students, teachers, and members of the community together through collaboration across state and national boundaries. This effort brought students, teachers, and community members in El Paso closer to their peers in the East Texas community of Sour Lake. During the past several years, the agency has provided support for other such projects tailored to specific needs by the classroom teacher. Examples of such projects include projects that enabled handicapped students to share their writing with other geographically dispersed students throughout the state and nation. In addition, the Induction Year pilot supported new teachers as they were inducted into the profession of teaching. Through a collaborative effort with educators in the state, the agency supports the use of telecommunications as an instructional application that extends learning beyond physical barriers and time constraints.

Telecomputing is an ongoing part of the institutional services offered to Texas educators. The challenge remains to continue the growing of the network from one that offers a dial-up service supporting individuals dialoguing directly with a remote host, to a service that facilitates peer networking. This is a network in which a teacher in a classroom may share files and resources with her/his colleagues' computers across the hall via a local area network or access the broader network and establish a peer relationship with colleagues. It is here that affiliation between the learner and the instructor change as each learns and instructs. The magnitude of providing such services in Texas is staggering, with more than 200,000 teachers and 3.2 million students. Technological, institutional, and financial barriers will need to be overcome. It will become a necessity to establish other partnerships that can support this type of relationship. The Texas Education Network as it is known in public education today is only in the initial stage of networking but as information technology expands, the potential is better understood.

References

Bull, Glen L., *et al.* "Public Education Network." Unpublished position paper, 1989.

Bull, Glen L., Harold Cothern, and Connie Stout. "Models for a national public school computing network." Paper presented at the Society for Technology and Teacher Education, March 1992.

Gore, Albert, Jr. "Viewpoint: A Networked Nation," *Communications of the Association for Computing* 34 (1991): 15–16.

Parker, C. "Technology and Telecommunications in Public Education." Texas Senate Bill 650, Section 14.042, 71st Legislature, May 1989.

Parker, C. Texas Senate Bill 1, Section 14.061, Sixth Called Session, 71st Legislature.

Parker, C. Texas Senate Bill 357, Regular Session, 72nd Legislature.

A Paradox for the Public Library

Bernard A. Margolis
Director, Pikes Peak Library District
Colorado Springs, Colorado

E xploring paradoxes is much like exploring a cave without a light. One
never knows all that is there to be seen, and one is probably better
off living with that ignorance. The paradox that I want to explore is
very much present in the world of public libraries. Bring your flashlight.
Increased demands for services, a public dying for material to read, students
as inquisitive as ever, and people living longer and reading longer have pro-
pelled many libraries, such as the Pikes Peak Library District, into an increased quest for additional materials. One of the Pikes Peak Library District's
strategic objectives for the past four years has been "books, books, and more
books." Along with this drive comes the inevitable demand for more library
facilities to house the expanding collections of materials. Library building and
construction activity continue at a hectic pace all across America.

On the other side of this paradox is the technological revolution that in
many libraries has already changed the manner in which libraries provide
information to their patrons. The famous psychologist Abraham Maslow
coined the appropriate phrase, "the same fire that melts the butter, hardens
the egg." The phrase is appropriate in further describing this paradox.
Libraries are running to increase their library materials, their books, magazines, videos, etc. and at the same time and with the same motivation, they
are working to tear down the walls by providing a new "virtual" access to
their storehouse of resources. The same motivation that propels libraries to
buy more books, to build more buildings, to have more things is also propelling them to use technology to reduce the size of reference collections

and to tear down the walls that on occasion have provided barriers to access. Many libraries are working to create an environment of "nothings." The paradox of wanting things and "no—things" at the same time will obviously remain with us. It is much like the fire that melts and softens and hardens at the same time.

To further view the obstacles in this paradox I invite you to ancient India. One of the most important Indian deities is Lord Ganesh. Best known as the elephant-headed man, Lord Ganesh is called on because he has special powers to remove obstacles. I have been told that on final exam day holy places throughout India dedicated to Lord Ganesh are filled with students seeking Ganesh's assistance in overcoming their obstacles and receiving passing grades. Visual characterizations of Lord Ganesh generally have him with at least four arms (and sometimes up to 118). In many ways he is like the modern computer, able to grab many things at once and able with just some keystrokes, to overcome barriers of distance and time in order to access information. It coincidentally is quite appropriate that Lord Ganesh relies heavily on a mouse to assist him in his task of removing and overcoming barriers. Could it be that this important deity helped with the invention of the computer and the mouse as we know it today? For purposes of this discussion Lord Ganesh is important because he symbolizes the movement towards the virtual library that is much with us now. It is with great reluctance that I use the word virtual, noting recently that it is a registered trademark of a high-tech product, nonetheless I will use it. As we move toward and embrace the concept of the virtual library, what we embrace most importantly is the concept of removing all obstacles. It is the absence of barriers of time and distance that make a library a virtual library. These obstacles are removed, not by ignoring their presence in the cave, but by actual and real removal. When we shine the flashlight on the process of creating the virtual library, what we see before us is mostly transparent. What we see is a means of sharing information without much regard to time or location. People have the information when and where they want it.

The Pikes Peak Library District is one public library dealing with the paradox noted earlier. As part of that "wrestling" process, it is moving toward providing a virtual library environment for the approximately 400,000 residents in the community that it serves. El Paso County, Colorado with its largest city, Colorado Springs, is unique not only for its location at the foot of world famous Pikes Peak but also for its long-term commitment and long-term pioneering efforts to use technology to improve public library services. The library district has experienced phenomenal growth with overall library use up fifteen percent over each of the last three years. Over 2.5 million items were borrowed in 1991, an increase of over seventeen percent from 1990. In the past four and a half years the library's collection has almost doubled, with the one millionth item just added to the collection.

The Pikes Peak Library District has attempted to respond to the significant increases in demand for books and more books. At the same time that it has increased its annual allocations for books and other materials, it also has instituted innovative services and programs. The library district has an active public programming agenda that includes programs for children as well as adults, a keen commitment to personalized service, a responsiveness to individual patron requests, and a spectacular computer system called MAGGIE'S PLACE. While the sluggish economy undoubtedly has had a positive impact on the significant increases in demand for all of the library's services, the typical roller coaster economy of Colorado has been so unpredictable that the effect is difficult to measure.

For many years, Colorado Springs has been known as "Silicon Mountain." This name came with the significant numbers of high technology firms in its community. Digital Equipment Corporation, Hewlett-Packard, Laser Magnetics, and a variety of other firms have all added to a sophisticated community clientele knowledgeable about computer technology and its ability to easily bring products to people's doors.

Many years ago the Pikes Peak Library District set out to be the information center for El Paso County. The library identified information as one of its most important and vital products. The shaping of MAGGIE'S PLACE attempted to respond from a service and need standpoint to patron interest and demands, and at the same time to remove as many barriers to access as possible. This movement toward a virtual library, accessible twenty-four hours a day and, of course, available free to all, first began in 1980. As with any library automation project, the library's first computer was intended, in part, to simplify and ease the costs associated with traditional library catalogs. It quickly grew beyond that by offering a dial-up, or a dial-in, service as one of its early components. With this service individuals, businesses, and corporations with computer dial-in capabilities could communicate with the library's computer system around the clock. Today we operate with twelve incoming lines that are constantly being used, indeed around the clock. For the Pikes Peak Library District the library quickly became more than just a physical place. It became an accessible service now usable by many more people in the community. By dialing into MAGGIE'S PLACE students, teachers, business people, researchers, and others have access to a wide array of information without leaving their desks or the comfort and convenience of their home or business. While daytime use is heavy with school and business connections, our evening hours also have significant demand. Calls are received every hour of the day and night, averaging 5,000 calls per month. If we had just an electronic card catalog, the merits and usefulness of this dial-in service might be diminished. We have in part attracted a loyal and consistent following because we offer much more than simply a catalog of the library's current holdings. Through the Colorado Alliance of Research

Libraries (CARL) and the network of other libraries participating with CARL, patrons now have access to an entire universe of library catalogs. And with those catalogs comes access to databases, full text services, and other useful indexes.

Through the Colorado Alliance of Research Libraries, a large number of Colorado institutions concentrated in the Denver metropolitan area are available for access. These range from the University of Colorado at Boulder to the Denver Public Library and also include the University of Wyoming Library System. These libraries provide access not only to their automated catalogs but also to other databases and services. In addition to the CARL libraries, other libraries that feed into the CARL system are also available, including the MARMOT system that includes dozens of libraries on Colorado's western slope and the Boulder Public Library. In addition, libraries in other states are accessible, including the Montgomery County (Maryland) public libraries; the University of Hawaii Library System; the Sno-Isle Regional Library in Marysville, Washington; the University of Maryland Library System; Arizona State University and Northern Arizona University, to name just a few. Access to all of these institutions is indeed available in the virtual environment. A few key strokes on the terminal or PC will access these, all free of charge.

One of the most important features of MAGGIE'S PLACE is called Community Connections. Community Connections is a bookshelf full of databases that are structured, organized, and compiled by the Pikes Peak Library District staff members in response to both general and specific needs identified in our unique community. Some of the databases were developed as an outgrowth of community studies and community planning. Citizens' Goals, an active community leadership organization, has worked closely with the library to identify areas in which easily accessible information resources were lacking. Many of the databases are intended to link citizens to resources that are either elusive or normally difficult to access.

Our first Community Connection is our community calendar database. The calendar lists events of all types in the Pikes Peak region, including public events, park and recreation events, concerts, lectures, our wonderful symphony programs, college events, the circus, and the world famous Olympic Training Center. The calendar is searchable both in the library and online from home or business by date, place, type of event, and contact person. We generally carry 600 to 700 items in this database. We use this database to produce an annual community calendar, which has become an important tool to assist all kinds of organizations in planning their own future activities and in coordinating activities with other groups and organizations.

In using the Community Calendar database, one needs simply to select "calendar" and to follow the menu available. The public terminal menus currently include seven primary options, including the Pikes Peak Library District's online catalog; our menu of community information databases; encyclopedia, business, and reference sources; magazine, journal, and newspaper indexes; menu of local government databases including city hall online; menu of other library systems; and help and library news. If one selects menu item 2, Community Connections, additional menu options appear headed off by database "54", our community calendar. Hitting "54" brings us to the Calendar database (see Exhibit A). The opening screen for the Calendar database informs us that we can find events listed both by name and by word. Names can be event dates, locations, sponsors, or even contact persons. Words can be titles, types of events, or any miscellaneous information. If we type a "W," we are asked, with examples, to include a word. In the example, we typed "Christmas" and were informed that there were eighty-three calendar items in the database that included Christmas activities. Exhibit B reveals just a sample of some of those calendar items. If we selected menu item 4, we would find information about an event entitled "Country Christmas at White House Ranch" with further information on that Christmas related event (see Exhibit C). At any time along the way we can type "help" and receive further instructional information to help us through this particular database or to direct us, if appropriate, to another Community Connections database that may be more appropriate to our specific needs. In each and every case, the purpose and approach is to move people methodically through the information sorting process to the information they desire.

Another part of our Community Connections bookshelf is our agency file. The Agencies database is much like a traditional information and referral database, which includes social service and community agencies publicly and privately supported. The database is searchable by word, name of the agency, and type of service. By typing in the word "counseling" or "food" or "housing," one will find a list of community counseling services, food banks, or housing services. The agency file also includes a comprehensive list of local officials both elected and appointed from all levels of local government including the city of Colorado Springs and El Paso County as well as our other municipal entities. This database, much like the Calendar database, currently includes close to 700 items.

The Agencies database is simply used. It includes access by name with inclusion of traditional agency names as well as more common names, parent organizations, agency directors and contact persons, as well as local officials. Word access to this database via name, agency function, keywords, and local officials' titles makes it extremely versatile to use. As with our other databases, there is a Browse function that permits people to scroll through the entire database. It is hoped that this process, similar to browsing at books on a shelf, might create some improved information access for

EXHIBIT A

WORKING . . .

                    SELECTED DATABASE: Calendar

The computer can find events by NAME or by WORD

NAMES can be event dates, event locations, event
     sponsors, or event contact persons.

WORDS can be event titles, event types, or
     miscellaneous information.

You may also BROWSE by event titles (TITLE).
     BROWSING by CALL NUMBER is not recommended.

Enter N for NAME search
       W for WORD search
       B to   BROWSE by title, series or call
               number
       S to   STOP or SWITCH to another Library
               catalog

Type the letter for the kind of search you want, and
     end each line you type by pressing <RETURN>
                 SELECTED DATABASE: Calendar

ENTER COMMAND (?H FOR HELP) >> w

REMEMBER—WORDS can be words from event titles, event
     types, or miscellaneous information.

          for example — PEACE PROSPECTS IN THE MIDDLE EAST
                        SEMINAR
                        SPEAKER JOHN DOE

Enter word or words (no more than one line, please)
separated by spaces and press <RETURN>.

>Christmas

WORKING . . .
CHRISTMAS   83 ITEMS

You may make your search more specific (and reduce the
size of the list) by adding another word to your
search. The result will be items in your current list
that also contain the new word.

   to ADD a new word, enter it,

   <D>ISPLAY to see the current list, or

   <Q>UIT for a new search:

NEW WORD(S): d

EXHIBIT B

```
1 Annually in december                   PPLD
    Christmas walk                        CALENDAR FILE

2 Annually in december                   PPLD
    Senior christmas dinner               CALENDAR FILE

3 Annually in december                   PPLD
    Victorian christmas in cripple creek  CALENDAR FILE

4 Annually in september                  PPLD
    Country christmas white house ranch   CALENDAR FILE

5 Annually in december                   PPLD
    A colorado christmas at the broadmoor CALENDAR FILE

6 Annually in december                   PPLD
    Christmas concert,                    CALENDAR FILE

7 Annually in november                   PPLD
    Black forest arts & crafts            CALENDAR FILE
```

```
<RETURN> TO CONTINUE DISPLAY
ENTER <LINE NUMBER(S)> TO DISPLAY FULL RECORDS
<P>REVIOUS FOR PREVIOUS PAGE OR <Q>UIT FOR NEW SEARCH 4
```

EXHIBIT C

```
-----------------------------Calendar---------------
AUTHOR(s):       ANNUALLY IN SEPTEMBER
TITLE(s):        Country Christmas At White House Ranch
                 SPONSOR: Holly Berry House
                 CONTACT: 633-2026

OTHER ENTRIES:   MISC: Annual event usually held the
                 third week of September.
                 DATE UPDATED: 06-OCT-92

CALL  #:  CALENDAR FILE                    LIBRARY:


----4 of 83--------------------Calendar---------------
<RETURN> to continue, <Q>UIT for a new search,
or <R>EPEAT this display, ? for HELP >
```

the user. If we pursue a word search of the Agencies database, we would be reminded of some examples of possible words to consider (see Exhibit D). And if we type a specific word, such as "hospice," we will find one agency listed in the file called Pikes Peak Hospice, Inc. If we look at Exhibit E, we will see a full review of this agency along with basic information about the organization as well as eligibility information and a more detailed review of its entire service list. Also noted will be other keywords under which this agency might be filed. These keywords, much like the tracings in card cat-

EXHIBIT D

SELECTED DATABASE: Agencies

The computer can find agencies or local officials by
NAME or by WORD.

NAMES can be agency names, parent organizations, agency
directors, contact persons, or local officials.

WORDS can be agency names, agency functions, keywords,
or local officials' titles.

You may also BROWSE by agency names (TITLE). BROWSING
by CALL NUMBER is not recommended.

```
Enter   N   for NAME search
        W   for WORD search
        B   to  BROWSE by title, series or call number
        S   to  STOP or SWITCH to another Library catalog
```

Type the letter for the kind of search you want,
and end each line you type by pressing <RETURN>
SELECTED DATABASE: Agencies

ENTER COMMAND (?H FOR HELP) >> w

REMEMBER — WORDS can be words from agency names, agency
functions and services, or keywords.

```
    for example —  SALVATION ARMY
                   ALCOHOLISM
                   MENTAL HEALTH
                   RUNAWAYS
```

Enter word or words (no more than one line, please)
separated by spaces and press <RETURN>.

>Hospice

```
WORKING . . .
HOSPICE                    1 ITEMS
1                                        PPLD
    Pikes peak hospice, inc.      AGENCY FILE
```

Enter <LINE NUMBER> to display full record, or <Q>UIT
for new search 1

alogs, might help individuals find other agencies that might provide them
with similar services. The Agencies database is updated regularly with assistance from our local United Way agency. As with all other databases, we
encourage people who may in some manner be listed in this database to
contact us with changes and updates, and we attempt to incorporate these
regularly. To guide both our staff and the public in using these databases,

EXHIBIT E

```
---------------------------------Agencies-----------
TITLE(s):       PIKES PEAK HOSPICE, INC.
```

ADDRESS: 3630 Sinton Road, Suite 302
CITY, ST, ZIP: Colorado Springs, CO
80907
HOURS: 8AM-5PM, M-F, office; A Hospice
physician and nurse are on-call to
patients and families 24 hours a day, 7
days a week.
TELEPHONE: 633-3400; Fax 633-1150
PARENT ORG: Pikes Peak Hospice, Inc.
DIRECTOR: Martha M. Barton
CONTACT: Carole Kingston Miller
PURPOSE: The Pikes Peak Hospice, Inc. is
a non-profit organization dedicated to
the care and support of persons with
terminal illness and their families.
Hospice also provides comprehensive
grief counseling, and
educational/informational services to El
Paso County residents and school
districts.

OTHER ENTRIES: SERVICES: Home Care: Provides necessary
support and medical services to make it
possible for patients to live out their
final months with the help of family
members in the comfort of their own
home; Hospice Care Facilities: For
patients who cannot remain at home
without a caregiver or when the
caregiver is no longer able to manage
the care; Regardless of the location in
El Paso County, Hospice provides visits
by a nurse, a home health aide, a
volunteer, a social worker and a
pastoral care worker as needed or
requested; in addition to the patient's
own doctor, Hospice physicians are
available.
ELIGIBILITY REQUIREMENTS: Pikes Peak
Hospice care is available to terminally
ill people of any age, with a life
expectancy of six months or less, who
are residents of El Paso County.
APPLICATION PROCEDURES: Physician
referral.
FEES: Sliding scale available; accept
Medicare, Medicaid, Champus

Exhibit E Continued

```
                    and private insurance;
                    financial assistance available.
                    FUNDING: Grants, donations, insurance
                    payments, Medicare, Medicaid, Champus;
                    non-profit.

                    KEYWORDS: DEATH GRIEF FAMILY
                    COUNSELING DISEASES HOME CARE DIR*
                    NOTES: Language interpreters available.
                    DATE ENTERED: 24-Aug-80
                    DATE UPDATED: 09-JUL-92
                    AGENCY: PIKES PEAK HOSPICE, INC.
CALL # AGENCY FILE                              LIBRARY:
---1 of 1-----------------Agencies-------------------
<RETURN> to continue, <Q>UIT for a new search, or
<R>EPEAT this display, ? for HELP >
```

we include the dates of the last agency update to give a gauge on the accuracy of the information provided.

Interested in computers or ham radios or western square dancing? Our Clubs database is a comprehensive listing of clubs of all types in the region. The file includes the club's purpose, meeting times, requirements (if any), dues, and general information on the club's purpose and focus. The file can be searched by the name of the club, its function, or basic type. This database currently includes close to 900 clubs in our region.

The extensive use of the Clubs database reflects significant interest on the part of our community in recreational and other ventures. The club file can be searched by names and words. The "word" search leads people by interest, area, as well as club names and functions. The "name" file includes club names, officers, and contact persons. This resource can be used by typing in a name and finding the various organizations that someone may be serving as an officer or contact person. In Exhibit F we were trying to find information about ham radio clubs and found that though "ham" is not in the database, "radio" appears three times. We found in this example that although "ham radio" is not a keyword, we still found the organizations that we were seeking which involve people in the amateur radio world. We zeroed in, particularly, on the second club listed and found more detailed information (see Exhibit G) on the Mountain Amateur Radio Club, also known as MARC. The information was last updated in March of 1992, and we had a teaser in the file that told us that in December of 1992 the information needed to be updated again.

While our traditional library does not deliver instruction or teaching, it does include a comprehensive database of courses. Courses included range

EXHIBIT F

```
WORKING . . .
                    SELECTED DATABASE: Clubs
    The computer can find clubs by NAME or by WORD

    NAMES can be club names, club officers, or
    contact persons.

    WORDS can be club names, club functions and
    interests, or keywords.

    You may also BROWSE by club names (TITLE).
    BROWSING by CALL NUMBER is not recommended.

    Enter   N   for   NAME search
            W   for   WORD search
            B   to    BROWSE by title, series or call
                      number
            S   to    STOP or SWITCH to another Library
                      catalog

    Type the letter for the kind of search you want,
    and end each line you type by pressing <RETURN>
                    SELECTED DATABASE: Clubs

ENTER COMMAND (?H FOR HELP) >> w

REMEMBER — WORDS can be words from club names, club
functions and interests, or keywords.

            for example — AUDUBON SOCIETY
                          SERVICE
                          BUSINESS
                          HIKING

Enter word or words (no more than one line, please)
separated by spaces and press <RETURN>.

>ham radio

WORKING . . .
HAM is not in the data base
RADIO       3 ITEMS

For the     3 items that have
RADIO
Press <RETURN>, or type <Q>UIT for a new search.
```

from those at colleges and universities to those conducted by the park and recreation department, clubs, and commercial establishments. Everything from computer classes, to quilting, and to the widest range of "how to do it" classes and courses imaginable, is listed. Our community's principal institutions of higher learning, including the University of Colorado at Colorado Springs, Pikes Peak Community College, Regis University, and

EXHIBIT G

1	PPLD —
React, inc. c-371, pikes peak region	CLUB FILE
2	PPLD —
Mountain amateur radio club (marc)	CLUB FILE
3	PPLD —
Marc (see) mountain amateur radio club	CLUB FILE

ALL ITEMS HAVE BEEN DISPLAYED.
ENTER <LINE NUMBER(S)> TO DISPLAY FULL RECORDS
<P>REVIOUS FOR PREVIOUS PAGE OR <Q>UIT FOR NEW SEARCH 2

------------------------Clubs------------------------
```
TITLE(s):      MOUNTAIN AMATEUR RADIO CLUB (MARC)

               ADDRESS: P.O. BOX 1012,
               ATTN: G. E. HINDS, N8C1X
               CITY, ST, ZIP: WOODLAND PARK, CO 80866
               MEMBERSHIP: 55 MEMBERS
               TELEPHONE: 684-2025. . . . 687-2146. . . .
               687-2610
               MEETINGS: 7:00 PM ON THIRD WEDNESDAY
               MONTHLY AT TELLER COUNTY OFFICE AT
               WOODLAND PARK.
               OFFICER: DON SWEARINGEN NOLHC,
               PRESIDENT. . . . 687-9641
               DAYTIME. . . . 687-9641
               CONTACT: GEORGE HINDS, N8CIX,
               EDITOR-PR REP. . . . 687-2610
               DAYTIME. . . . 687-2610 EVENING

OTHER ENTRIES: FUNCTION: ENCOURAGE INTEREST IN
               RADIO/ELECTRONICS THROUGH THE AMATEUR
               RADIO SERVICE; SERVICE TO PUBLIC
               AGENCIES IN EMERGENCIES, ETC.
               APPLICATION: ANNUAL MEMBERSHIP DUES OF
               $12.00 ($12.00 ADDITIONAL FOR AUTOPATCH
               USE)
               KEYWORDS: DECEMBER RADIO LICENSED
               AMATEUR OPERATORS ELECTRONICS
               COMMUNICATIONS
               DATE ENTERED: 16-JAN-90
               DATE UPDATED: 20-MAR-92
               RENEW DATE: DEC 92
               CLUB: MOUNTAIN AMATEUR RADIO CLUB (MARC)

CALL # CLUB FILE                               LIBRARY:
----2 of 7-------------------Clubs--------------------
<RETURN> to continue, <Q>UIT for a new search,
or <R>EPEAT this display, ? for HELP >
```

Blair Junior College, have their courses included. This database currently includes almost 1,300 items. Assigned to all of the databases is a library staff member assisted by a library paraprofessional. Their assignment principally includes capturing the often elusive information required to keep the databases up-to-date as well as deleting outdated information and making suggestions for improving the scope and comprehensiveness of the database.

The Courses database works in much the same way as our other databases. "Name" access includes locations, course identification numbers, sponsoring organizations, as well as the names of formal and popular schools offering the various courses. "Word" access includes course title, subject, and keyword. In our example (see Exhibit H) we selected a word search on the subject of pottery and found three items listed. One was an open studio for potters, the other, clay/beginning wheelthrowing, and the third was an additional course on wheelthrowing. Zeroing in more specifically on the clay/beginning wheelthrowing course, we found that it is being offered by Bemis Art School. Included are its cost and location and a basic course description (see Exhibit I). If we followed with a name search using Bemis Art School as the name, we would find not only this pottery course but a variety of other courses that might be of interest to the inquiring patron. We have attempted to interrelate the search methodologies so that people can use a variety of different approaches and achieve success in finding the desired information.

Our Local Authors database developed out of our own need to document the written heritage of our community and to capture in one place information on all of the authors residing in the Pikes Peak Region. The Local Authors database has become an excellent community speakers' bureau with many organizations relying on the database as a good place to find a speaker for an event or on a specific topic. We currently list 163 local authors. New authors are constantly added. An annual questionnaire sent to all the authors guarantees accuracy of the information included.

The Local Authors Database is often used as a tool for the library's own programming activities. While the database is generally used with name access, it also provides word access. The word access can be the title of a work, a general subject, publication date, or a more general idea. Access by name includes authors, editors, as well as names of persons or institutions written about in a book. In our example (see Exhibit J) we use the name Donna Guthrie. Guthrie is a member of the board of trustees of the Pikes Peak Library District and a well-known children's author. The database does show a listing for Donna W. Guthrie, and further review (see Exhibit K) shows the full file on Guthrie with mailing address and telephone contact number. It also includes a list of her publications awards and honors. Although this is updated by our annual questionnaire, our staff also updates this file from their general and professional knowledge.

EXHIBIT H

WORKING . . .

SELECTED DATABASE: Courses

The computer can find courses by NAME or by WORD.

NAMES can be course identification numbers,
locations, names of sponsors, or names and
pseudonyms of schools.

WORDS can be course titles, content, or keywords.

You may also BROWSE by course titles or institutions
(TITLE).

This information is offered to you as a service.
However, the Pikes Peak Library District cannot be
responsible for the accuracy of times, dates and
course offerings.

```
Enter  N  for  NAME search
       W  for  WORD search
       B  to   BROWSE by title or call number
       S  to   STOP or SWITCH to another Library
              catalog
```

Type the letter for the kind of search you want and
press <RETURN>
SELECTED DATABASE: Courses

ENTER COMMAND (?H FOR HELP) >> w

REMEMBER—WORDS can be words from course titles,
content, or keywords.

```
for example — CAREER DEVELOPMENT
              SPANISH
              COMPUTER FORTRAN
```

Enter word or words (no more than one line, please)
separated by spaces and press <RETURN>.

>pottery

WORKING . . .
POTTERY   3 ITEMS
1 Course   PPLD   —
   Open studio for potters   COURSES

2 Course   PPLD   —
   Clay/beginning wheelthrowing COURSES

3 Course   PPLD   —
   Wheelthrowing   COURSES

EXHIBIT I

```
ALL ITEMS HAVE BEEN DISPLAYED.
ENTER <LINE NUMBER(S)> TO DISPLAY FULL RECORDS (Number
+ B for Brief)
<P>REVIOUS FOR PREVIOUS PAGE OR <Q>UIT FOR NEW SEARCH 2

----------------------------Courses------------------
AUTHOR(s):      COURSE
TITLE(s):       CLAY/BEGINNING WHEELTHROWING

                FROM-TO: JUNE 16-JULY 23, 1992
                DAYS: TUESDAY, THURSDAY
                HOURS: 4:00PM-6:00PM
                COST: $96.00 + $12.00 LAB FEE
                TELEPHONE: 475-2444
                LOCATION: BEMIS ART SCHOOL
                ADDRESS: 30 W. DALE
                CITY, ST, ZIP: COLORADO SPRINGS, CO

OTHER ENTRIES: MISC. INFO: RECEIVE INDIVIDUAL
                INSTRUCTION FOR USING THE POTTER'S WHEEL
                AND LEARNING GLAZING AND DECORATIVE
                TECHNIQUES. GLAZES AND FIRINGS PROVIDED.
                KEYWORDS: BA1 POTTERY JUNE ADULT
                DATE ENTERED: 15-JUN-92

CALL # COURSES                          LIBRARY:

---2 of 3------------------Courses-------------------
<RETURN> to continue, <Q>UIT for a new search,
or <R>EPEAT this display, ? for HELP >
```

One of the most exciting and intriguing databases that we maintain is called our Social and Economic Indicators database. With almost 600 items included, this database includes a wide variety of information tables in over fifty categories about the Pikes Peak region, with comparisons to other parts of the United States. Topics include everything from snowfall to salaries to transportation to foreclosures to census data to housing starts to real estate profiles to types of commercial and retail stores. The list goes on and is used heavily by our economic development community as well as by people interested in relocating to Colorado Springs, starting businesses, or simply in finding the best school district for their children. Because much of this information is pulled from printed sources, this database does provide citations for all of the information tables included.

The opening screen for the Social and Economic Indicator database, as with our other databases, includes the usual name and word search. It also

EXHIBIT J

WORKING . . .

SELECTED DATABASE: Local Authors

The computer can find items by NAME or by WORD

NAMES can be authors, editors, or names of persons or institutions written about in the book.

WORDS can be words from the title, or subjects, concepts, ideas, dates etc.

You may also BROWSE by TITLE, CALL NUMBER, or SERIES.

Enter N for NAME search
       W for WORD search
       B to   BROWSE title, call number, or series
       S to   STOP or SWITCH to another database

Type the letter for the search you want, and press <RETURN>, or type ? for <HELP>
SELECTED DATABASE: Local Authors

ENTER COMMAND (?H FOR HELP) >> n
SELECTED DATABASE: Local Authors

REMEMBER — NAMES can be authors, editors, or names of persons or institutions
written about in the book.

for example — items   BY   WILLIAM FAULKNER
               items   BY   SALINGER, J. D.
               items   BY   XEROX

or   — items   ABOUT   JOHN KENNEDY
               items   ABOUT   EASTMAN KODAK
               items   ABOUT   VIRGINIA WOOLF

Enter NAMES (in any order) on one line, separated by spaces.

>guthrie, donna

WORKING . . .
GUTHRIE   1 NAME
GUTHRIE + DONNA   1

Author: Guthrie, Donna W
  1 ITEM
    1 Author guthrie donna   PPLD
       Occupation: freelance writer AU-0023/072689

EXHIBIT K

```
Enter <LINE NUMBER> to display full record,
or <Q>UIT for new search 1

-----------------------Local Authors----------------
AUTHOR(s):      AUTHOR: Guthrie, Donna W.
TITLE(s):       OCCUPATION: Freelance Writer
                TOPICS: Children's Stories
                PUBLICATIONS: BOOKS: The Witch Who Lives
                Down The Hall, 1985; Grandpa Doesn't
                Know It's Me, 1986; This Little Pig
                Stayed Home, 1987; While I'm Waiting,
                1988; A Rose For Abby, 1988; Mrs.
                GiggleBelly Is Coming For Tea, 1990; The
                Witch Has An Itch, 1990
                AVAILABLE FOR SEMINAR/WORKSHOP
                   SPEAKER: No
                AWARDS, HONORS: Junior Literary Guild
                Selection and Book of the Month Club
                Selection for THE WITCH WHO LIVES DOWN
                THE HALL

OTHER ENTRIES: EDUCATION, TRAINING: Bachelor of Arts in
                Journalism, Rider College, 1968
                PLACE, DATE OF BIRTH: Washington,
                Pennsylvania; 5/15/46
                MAILING ADDRESS: 15 East Fontanero,
                Colorado Springs, CO 80907
                TELEPHONE: 471-9067

CALL # AU-0023/072689                    LIBRARY:

---1 of 1--------------------Local Authors------------
<RETURN> to continue, <Q>UIT for a new search,
or <R>EPEAT this display, ? for HELP >
```

includes a note of encouragement that because of the nature of this statistical information users are encouraged to consult the actual source listed on the informational records (see Exhibit L). We selected, in this particular case, the words "high school" and determined that five entries include information relative to high schools in the community (see Exhibit M). We hit entry "2," which took us to an extensive entry that shows average test scores, high school graduation rates, dropout rates, as well as other information about our community schools, including seventeen area high schools (see Exhibit N). The information came from a local newspaper report that was added to the database in March of 1992. While "high school" is not listed as a keyword, it certainly is the subject of much of the information included in this entry.

EXHIBIT L

```
WORKING . . .
          SELECTED DATABASE: Social and Economic
    The computer can find statistics by WORD or by NAME.
    WORDS can be subjects, topics, ideas, or keywords.
    NAMES can be sources, such as books, documents,
       authors, or institutions from which the
       statistics are gathered.
    You may also obtain an alphabetical listing of the
       entries in this database by doing a BROWSE by
       (TITLE).
    WORD searching works best . . .

    Enter  N  for  NAME search
           W  for  WORD search
           B  to   BROWSE by <T>itle
           S  to   STOP or SWITCH to other Library
                   catalog

The Social and Economic Indicators database is a
compilation of statistical information from a variety
of external sources. The Library attempts to include
the most accurate and most current information
available. Users are encouraged to consult the source
listed on the record for additional information.

Type the letter for the kind of search you want, and
press <RETURN>
          SELECTED DATABASE: Social and Economic

ENTER COMMAND (?H FOR HELP) >> w

REMEMBER—WORDS can be subjects, topics, ideas, or
keywords.
          for example — POPULATION
                        EL PASO COUNTY
                        APARTMENT RENTAL PRICES
```

Our Local Documents database includes an annotated index to virtually all of the documents and publications issued by governmental bodies in El Paso County and adjoining Teller County. If you are looking for a city charter, a local air pollution quality control plant, bidding documents for a new bridge, or anything else that might have been generated with tax money, this is the place to find it. The information comes from cities, counties, water districts, transportation plans, and the regional council of governments among others. This database now has over 4,000 items and is growing rapidly.

The Local Documents database has been an effective way to keep track of local government information including information about various agen-

EXHIBIT M

```
Enter word or words (no more than one line, please)
separated by spaces and press <RETURN>.

>high school

WORKING . . .
HIGH 15 ITEMS
HIGH + SCHOOL      5 ITEMS

Set of 5 will display on one page—proceeding with
display . . .

1                              PPLD                 —
District 11 profile (1990)     SOCIAL & ECONOMIC

2                              PPLD                 —
Education stats-local/state/   SOCIAL & ECONOMIC
nat'l-1991

3                              PPLD                 —
Private schools (1990)         SOCIAL & ECONOMIC

4                              PPLD                 —
Profile of school district 20  SOCIAL & ECONOMIC
(1988-89)

5                              PPLD                 —
Theaters and auditoriums       SOCIAL & ECONOMIC

ALL ITEMS HAVE BEEN DISPLAYED.
ENTER <LINE NUMBER(S)> TO DISPLAY FULL RECORDS
<P>REVIOUS FOR PREVIOUS PAGE OR <Q>UIT FOR NEW SEARCH 2
```

cies as well as about people in government. The word access to this database includes access by subject, concept, geographic areas, type of document or government publication, as well as by elected officials' titles (see Exhibit O). We chose a name search (see Exhibit P) looking for Marcy Morrison. We found that her name appeared twice. We chose the second entry and found her local street address and the information that she is an elected member of the board of county commissioners. One of the principal uses of this database is for people seeking information about individual elected officials in all parts of local government.

The Arts database is the newest member of the Community Connections database family. The need for this database grew out of our library's own extensive programming work. The Pikes Peak Library District is now one of four national sites that host the John F. Kennedy Center for the Performing Art's annual Imagination Celebration. This month-long series of art activities provides a great deal of attention to the library district and at the same time showcases the imagination and creativity of people in our community. In

EXHIBIT N

```
--------------------------Social and Economic---------
TITLE(s):        EDUCATION STATISTICS-LOCAL/STATE/NAT'L-1991
OTHER ENTRIES:        Pikes Peak Region  Colorado  U.S.
         ACT*                 22.2          21.3   20.6
         SAT Verbal**         474           453    422
         SAT Math**           528           506    474
         *All 10 districts reported scores.
         **Six of the 10 local districts reported scores.

         Area Graduation Rate: 82% (grades 9-12)
         Colorado Graduation Rate: 78.9% (grades 10-12)
         Percent of students going on to post-secondary
         education: 65%
         Area Drop-out Rate: 4% (Colorado: 4.8%)
         Colorado expenditure per pupil in 1989:
         $5,374.40
         (State data not available for 1990).
         Pikes Peak area expenditure per pupil in 1990:
         $4,117.00
         More than $25 million in scholarships offered
         to area seniors in 1991 graduating class.

         In October 1991, the Pikes Peak Area had:
         89 elementries
         26 middle schools or junior highs
         17 high schools
         71,570 students
         4,166 teachers
         A 17-to-1 students to teacher ratio
         (Includes SPEC teachers and teachers of
         specialized areas such as music, art, P.E., etc
```

The Pikes Peak area school districts included in the above statistics are: Academy School District 20, Cheyenne Mountain School District 12, Colorado Springs School District 11, Falcon School District 49, Fountain/Fort Carson School District 8, Harrison School District 2, Lewis-Palmer School District 38, Manitou Springs School District 14, Widefield School District 3, Woodland School District RE-2.

```
         SOURCE: Gazette Telegraph, February, 23, 1992.
            File added
               March, 1992.
            KEYWORDS: EDUCATION COLORADO SPRINGS
            SAT/ACT SCORES

     CALL # SOCIAL & ECONOMIC LIBRARY:

     ---2 of 5--------------------Social and Economic-------
```

EXHIBIT O

```
WORKING . . .

        SELECTED DATABASE: Local Documents

    The computer can find documents or elected
    officials by NAME or by WORD.

    NAMES can be authors, agencies, editors,
    consultants, or name of persons or institutions
    written about in the document.

    WORDS can be keywords from the title, abstract, or
    subjects, concepts, geographic areas, document
    types, dates, or elected officials' titles, etc.

    You may also BROWSE by document TITLE or by CALL
    NUMBER.

    Enter N for NAME search
          W for WORD search
          B to  BROWSE by title, series or call number
          S to  STOP or SWITCH to other Library catalog

    Type the letter for the kind of search you want,
    and end each line you type by pressing <RETURN>
        SELECTED DATABASE: Local Documents

ENTER COMMAND (?H FOR HELP) >> n

REMEMBER—NAMES can be agencies, authors, editors,
consultants, or names of persons or institutions
written about in the document.

for example
  — documents BY PIKES PEAK AREA COUNCIL OF GOVERNMENTS
    documents BY CHAMBER OF COMMERCE

  — documents ABOUT PARK AND RECREATION
    documents ABOUT LAND USE
```

1992 approximately 150,000 people participated in the events connected with the Imagination Celebration. Our own need to identify individual artists, included among others, painters and sculptors as well as performing artists, provoked our creation of this database. It can be used for everything from locating a magician to perform at a child's birthday party to finding information about a gallery or theater box office. For every artist seeking an audience, either to sell a painting or to seek a performance engagement, this database provides the necessary connections.

This database is a little more complex to use (see Exhibit Q) because there are many more access options. Name access includes one of five cat-

EXHIBIT P

```
Enter NAMES (in any order) on one line, separated by
spaces.

>MARCY MORRISON

WORKING . . .
MARCY        2 NAMES
MARCY + MORRISON  2


1 Additional authors: marcy morrison
    1 ITEM

2 Commissioner dist. 3: marcy morrison (r) 302
  sutherland pl.,
    1 ITEM

ALL ITEMS HAVE BEEN DISPLAYED.
ENTER <LINE NUMBER(S)> TO SELECT NAME(S)—(separate
numbers with commas) <Q>UIT FOR NEW SEARCH.2

Commissioner district 3: marcy morrison (r) 302
sutherland pl.,
1 ITEM
 1                            PPLD PENROS LOHIST —
   How to contact your local  COUNTY OFFICIALS
   elected

Enter <LINE NUMBER> to display full record, or <Q>UIT
for new search 1

---------------------Local Documents------------------
COMMISSIONER DISTRICT 3: Marcy Morrison (R)
302 Sutherland Pl., Manitou Springs, CO 80829 685-5929;
Elected to the Board of County Commissioners in 1984.
District includes southwest El Paso County.

---1 of 1------------------Local Documents-----------
<RETURN> to continue, <Q>UIT for a new search,
or <R>EPEAT this display, ? for HELP >
```

egories including visual artist, performing artist, visual space, performance place, or art organization. If you simply type the capital letter "N," you can type in a zip code and find listings for any of those five categories in your own neighborhood. Word access is the most common form of access to this database. This access includes names of artists, names of performers, arts organizations, art mediums, types of performances, types of visual space, types of performance places, and a large variety of other keywords includ-

EXHIBIT Q

WORKING . . .

SELECTED DATABASE: Arts Database

The computer can find items by using 2 commands: W or N

W can be name of artist, name of performer, arts organization, art medium, type of performance, type of visual space, type of performance place, and many other keywords indicating function, name, or service.

N can be zipcode NUMBER and/or NAME of 1 of 5 categories: Visual Artist; Performing Artist; Visual Space; Performance Places; Arts Organizations.

S to Stop or Switch to another database.

Enter W, N or S at the prompt.

SELECTED DATABASE: Arts Database

ENTER COMMAND (?H FOR HELP) >> w

The W command can be name of artist, name of performer, arts organization, art medium, type of performance, type of visual space, type of performance place, and many other keywords.
For example:

name of artist/s	Michael Garman
	Watercolor Society
name of performer/s	Patti Smith
	Rocky Mountain Cloggers
arts organization/s	Arts Council
	Symphony Guild
art medium	painting
	quilting
type of performance	jazz
	clown
type of visual space	gallery
	darkroom
type performance place	auditorium
	practice room
other keywords	box office
	theater

Enter word or words (on one line) separated by spaces and press <RETURN>

ing box office and theater (see Exhibit Q). In our example (see Exhibit R) we were looking for a cartoonist and found three individual cartoonists listed. In looking at the first one listed, we found out basic information including how to contact her and that her disciplines included not only cartooning but also graphic arts and pastel painting.

Our Senior Housing database came about when a variety of community organizations providing services to senior citizens identified a need for greater ease in locating available housing for older citizens. The database provides not only access to nursing homes but to all sorts and types of senior housing options, including residential housing. We find this database is often used by people as an aide to find suitable housing when considering retiring here. The database can be searched by street name, zip code, or type of service. In our example (see Exhibit S) we proceeded with a word search to find facilities that served people with low income. We found six items listed and selected Crestview (see Exhibit T). Crestview is operated by the Colorado Springs Housing Authority and provides housing for people meeting low income requirements of no more than $11,900 a year in income for one person. The information provided (see Exhibit U) includes other amenities and services that are offered at Crestview. Our staff updates this information periodically to guarantee its accuracy and its usefulness.

Our last Community Connections database is of Child Care Providers. This database is based on licenses of child care providers that is available as public information both through the state of Colorado and the El Paso County Department of Social Services (see Exhibit V). We decided to only include licensed child care providers so as not to appear to give information that is contrary to provisions of state law which require licensing for facilities handling child care.

A word search in the Child Care Providers database can include zip codes, neighborhoods, or the names of the nearest elementary school. Keywords, such as infant, part-time, or various days of the week, will also assist someone using this database in getting the needed information. Using a word search for Village Seven (see Exhibit W), a well-known Colorado Springs neighborhood, shows thirty-three items listed. Arbitrarily picking entry 5 (see Exhibit X) we find information on Adelia Okvath-Paul who serves the Village Seven area and has the capacity for five children in her home.

In addition to our Community Connections we have developed another interesting and unique series of databases focused on local government information. We explained the Agencies database earlier, which includes access to information on our elected officials. In addition to that database we also have the El Paso Legislative database. This database provides county precinct and district numbers for the United States Congress, state senate

EXHIBIT R

```
>CARTOONIST

WORKING . . .
CARTOONIST            3 ITEMS
1                                    Visual artists
    Wood, linda g.                   ARTS

2                                    Visual artists
    Maceachern, charlie              ARTS

3                                    Visual artists
    Cordtz, kevin                    ARTS
ALL ITEMS HAVE BEEN DISPLAYED.
ENTER <LINE NUMBER(S)> TO DISPLAY FULL RECORDS
<P>REVIOUS FOR PREVIOUS PAGE OR <Q>UIT FOR NEW SEARCH 1

----------------------Arts Database-----------------
                 Visual Artists
TITLE(s):        Wood, Linda G.
                 AFFILIATION: *
                 CONTACT:     *

                 ADDRESS:      5664 Corinth Dr.
                 CITY, STATE:  Colorado Springs, CO
                 ZIP:          80918
                 TELEPHONE:    531-7823

OTHER ENTRIES:   TYPE: Individual
                 DISCIPLINE: Graphic Artist, Pastel
                 Painter, Cartoonist
                 AVAILABLE FOR: Exhibits, private
                 consignments
                 FEES: Call for details
                 COMMENTS: Has appeared in many shows
                 locally and nationwide. Has received
                 many awards and honors. Resume
                 available. Art work has been published
                 in magazines and posters.

CALL #: ARTS                          LIBRARY:

----1 of 3-------------------Arts Database------------
<RETURN> to continue, <Q>UIT for a new search,
or <R>EPEAT this display, ? for HELP >
```

and representative districts, county commission districts, and local school districts. Typing in your street address will give you the information on your precinct and district and also the polling places for primary and general elections for all the governmental units that serve your particular address. This

EXHIBIT S

WORKING . . .

SELECTED DATABASE: Senior Housing

The computer can find housing options by NAME or by
WORD

NAMES can be facility names, types of facility,
facility administrators, or facility managers.

WORDS can be facility names, facility services and
descriptions, facility locations, or keywords.

You may also BROWSE by facility names (TITLE).
BROWSING by CALL NUMBER is not recommended.

```
Enter  N for NAME search
       W for WORD search
       B to  BROWSE by title, series or call number
       S to  STOP or SWITCH to another Library
             catalog
```

Type the letter for the kind of search you want,
and end each line you type by pressing <RETURN>
SELECTED DATABASE: Senior Housing

ENTER COMMAND (?H FOR HELP) >> W

REMEMBER—WORDS can be words from facility names, type
of facility, facility location, services provided, or
keywords.

```
for example — facility   NAME       BROOKSIDE SENIOR
                                    RESIDENCE
               facility   TYPE       RESIDENTIAL HOUSING
               facility   SERVICES   MEALS
                                    TRANSPORTATION
               facility   AMENITIES  HOUSEKEEPING
               facility   COST       LOW-INCOME
               facility   LOCATION   NORTH
                                    SOUTH
                                    EAST
                                    NORTHEAST
                                    SOUTHWEST
                                    CENTRAL
```

database also serves another interesting and important function in that it is
a zip code directory. Type any address and the database will also reveal the
zip code for that address (see Exhibit Y).

As part of our Local Government databases, we also have "City Hall On-
Line" (see Exhibit Z). This database is a joint project with the City of
Colorado Springs and the Pikes Peak Library District. It is constantly updated

EXHIBIT T

Enter word or words (no more than one line, please)
separated by spaces and press <RETURN>.

>LOW INCOME

WORKING . . .
LOW   7 ITEMS
LOW + INCOME   6 ITEMS

For the   6 items that have
LOW + INCOME
Press <RETURN>, or type <Q>UIT for a new search.

1	Residential housing Calhan housing authority	PPLD SENIOR HOUSING	—
2	Residential housing Crestview	PPLD SENIOR HOUSING	—
3	Residential housing Sunnyrest villa	PPLD SENIOR HOUSING	—
4	Residential housing Housing authority colorado springs	PPLD SENIOR HOUSING	—
5	Residential housing Eastborough village	PPLD SENIOR HOUSING	—
6	Residential housing Grinde manor	PPLD SENIOR HOUSING	—

ALL ITEMS HAVE BEEN DISPLAYED.
ENTER <LINE NUMBER(S)> TO DISPLAY FULL RECORDS
<P>REVIOUS FOR PREVIOUS PAGE OR <Q>UIT FOR NEW SEARCH 2

EXHIBIT U

---------------------Senior Housing-----------------
AUTHOR(s): RESIDENTIAL HOUSING
TITLE(s):   CRESTVIEW
            ADDRESS: 3880 VAN TEYLINGEN
            CITY/STATE/ZIP: COLORADO SPRINGS, CO 80917

            TELEPHONE: 578-6653; 578-6690;
            TDD 578-6749 (HOUSING AUTHORITY)
            ADMINISTRATOR/MANAGER: MARIE PUTERBAUGH,
            CORPORATE OWNER: HOUSING AUTHORITY
            CORPORATE ADDRESS: 30 SOUTH NEVADA SUITE
            304. CSC 80903
            PHYSICAL DESCRIPTION: 3-STORY SENIOR
            RESIDENCE BUILDING WITH 60 UNITS. BUILDING
            IS HANDICAPPED ACCESSIBLE WITH RAMPS AND
            ELEVATORS.

EXHIBIT U CONTINUED

MANAGED BY THE HOUSING AUTHORITY.
COST: LOW INCOME: 30% OF APPLICANTS
INCOME. RENT INCLUDES
UTILITIES. REFUNDABLE DEPOSIT REQUIRED.
A 30-DAY LEASE IS REQUIRED.
ENTRANCE REQUIREMENTS: APPLICANTS MUST MEET
LOW-INCOME REQUIREMENTS OF NO MORE THAN
$11,900/YEAR FOR 1 PERSON OR $13,600/YEAR
FOR 2 PERSONS. ENTRANCE RESTRICTIONS:
WAITING LIST

OTHER ENTRIES: SERVICES:
MAINTENANCE
RECREATIONAL ACTIVITIES
WEEKDAY NOON MEALS ARE PROVIDED BY THE
GOLDEN CIRCLE NUTRITION PROGRAM FOR AN
ADDITIONAL COST.
AMENITIES:
   LAUNDRY FACILITIES
   PARKING
BACKGROUND INFORMATION: AVERAGE AGE OF
RESIDENTS IS 73. HOUSING IS GEARED TOWARDS
PERSONS WHO ARE AT LEAST 62 YEARS OF AGE OR
HANDICAPPED/DISABLED.
NOTES: HUD SUBSIDIZED.
SEE OTHER ENTRIES: HOUSING AUTHORITY OF THE
CITY OF COLORADO SPRINGS.
FACILITY DESCRIPTOR: RESIDENTIAL HOUSING
LOCATION: NORTHEAST
DATE ENTERED: MAY 1988
DATE UPDATED: JUNE 1992
FACILITY NAME: CRESTVIEW

CALL #: SENIOR HOUSING   LIBRARY:

----2 of 6--------------------Senior Housing----------
<RETURN> to continue, <Q>UIT for a new search,
or <R>EPEAT this display, ? for HELP >

to include current news releases from the City of Colorado Springs as well as city council agendas and minutes and a comprehensive city source telephone directory. We did a subject search in the City News Releases under "cable television" (see Exhibit AA) and found information about the cable television advisory committee from a recent city news release.

And if that is not enough, we also offer to our virtual library users three other informational databases including the *Grolier's Academic Encyclopedia*, which includes over twenty volumes in a full-text format that

EXHIBIT V

```
WORKING . . .
          SELECTED DATABASE: Child Care Providers
```

The CHILD CARE database contains information about licensed child care services in El Paso County.

The following list of licensed providers is public information supplied by the State of Colorado and the El Paso County Department of Social Services. The Library is dependent on these agencies for accurate and current information. Inclusion in this list is voluntary and does not indicate or imply an endorsement by the Pikes Peak Library District, the State of Colorado, or El Paso County.

Use a WORD search to find child care services. For additional help type
S <RETURN> and the number preceding HELP on the menu, or please ask the Information and Reference staff or call 531-6333.

```
     Enter    W    for WORD search
              S    to STOP or SWITCH to another Library
                   catalog
```

Type the letter for the kind of search you want and press <RETURN>.

```
          SELECTED DATABASE: Child Care Providers
```

ENTER COMMAND (?H FOR HELP) >> w

```
WORDS can be elementary schools, neighborhoods, zip
      codes, or keywords which describe special
      features such as INFANTS, PART-TIME, and
      SATURDAYS. For a complete list of keywords,
      please refer to the HELP selection on the menu.

               for example — MONROE
                             80910
                             RUSTIC HILLS
                             INFANTS
```

is easily accessed by subject. Additionally, we have a weekly updated version of *Facts on File*, which includes national and international news from a wide variety of sources. This database is heavily used by our home users and in a short period of time has become one of our most popular databases.

In conjunction with the Colorado State Library, we also offer online the *Directory of Environmental Education* (DEER). This online directory includes organizations involved in environmental issues and provides general

EXHIBIT W

Enter word or words (no more than one line, please)
separated by spaces and press <RETURN>.

>Village Seven

WORKING . . .
VILLAGE   38 ITEMS
VILLAGE + SEVEN   33 ITEMS

For the   33 items that have
VILLAGE + SEVEN
Press <RETURN>, or type <Q>UIT for a new search.

VILLAGE + SEVEN   33 ITEMS

You may make your search more specific (and reduce the
size of the list) by adding another word to your
search. The result will be items in your current list
that also contain the new word.

to ADD a new word, enter it,

<D>ISPLAY to see the current list, or

<Q>UIT for a new search:

NEW WORD(S): d
  1 Burt bonnie   PPLD   —
    80917 barnes rd. & oro blanco CHILD CARE FILE

  2 Gray deanna   PPLD   —
    80917 n. carefree & oro blanco CHILD CARE FILE

  3 Horvath susan   PPLD   —
    80917 s. carefree & oro blanco CHILD CARE FILE

  4 Howell cheryl   PPLD   —
    80917 carefree & oro blanco   CHILD CARE FILE

  5 Okvath paul adelia   PPLD   —
    80917 carefree & austin bluffs CHILD CARE FILE

  6 Ortivez rose marie   PPLD   —
    80917 oro blanco & n. carefree CHILD CARE FILE

  7 Richardson lena   PPLD   —
    80917 artistic & oro blanco   CHILD CARE FILE

   <RETURN> TO CONTINUE DISPLAY
ENTER <LINE NUMBER(S)> TO DISPLAY FULL RECORDS Brief)
<P>REVIOUS FOR PREVIOUS PAGE OR <Q>UIT FOR NEW SEARCH 5

EXHIBIT X

```
------------------Child Care Providers---------------
AUTHOR(s):      OKVATH-PAUL, ADELIA
TITLE(s):       80917 N. Carefree & Austin Bluffs,
                Village Seven area
                CITY, ST., ZIP: Colorado Springs, CO
                80917
                ELEMENTARY SCHOOL: Carver

                TELEPHONE: 574-9568, call during the day
                TOTAL CAPACITY: 5 children + 1 b/a
                school
                OPEN: 7:00 am-5:30 pm Mon-Fri
                AGES: 1-16 years

OTHER ENTRIES: FEATURES: Before & after school care,
                hours by arrangement, flexible hours,
                toddlers, drop-ins, part-time care.
                Vacancies for 2 over 2 for fall '92.
                (home) (P)
                DIRECTOR: Adelia Okvath-Paul
                RENEWAL DATE: 07-Sep-93
                DATE UPDATED: 24-Jun-92

CALL #: CHILD CARE FILE                      LIBRARY:

----5 of 33---------------Child Care Providers---------
<RETURN> to continue, <Q>UIT for a new search,
or <R>EPEAT this display, ? for HELP >
```

organizational descriptions as well as contact persons and addresses and phone numbers.

In order to move along with the process of creating our virtual library, we also, from time to time, mount short-term databases that focus on current informational needs in our community. During the 1992 general election, we provided online, full text of the more than one dozen state and local ballot issues for voter view. In addition, we included full-text versions of legislative analyses of each ballot issue. This information proved to be quite helpful for our staff and for the public. We also added to the El Paso County Legislative District information an up-to-date database that provides voter news from the El Paso county clerk and recorder's office about various election matters. We expect from time to time to add other similar databases to meet community informational needs.

This is just a small glimpse of what the flashlight might reveal about the Pikes Peak Library District's cave of information. Operating with the Tandem CLX computer, we are able to expand even further our vision and perspective of a library district brimming over with books and at the same time pro-

EXHIBIT Y

Enter the NUMBER of your choice, and press the <RETURN>
key >> 52
WORKING . . .

SELECTED DATABASE: El Paso Legislative

This database provides El Paso County precinct and
district numbers for the U. S. Congress, State Senate
and Representative, County Commissioner & school
districts. The polling place for primary and general
elections covering county, state and federal officials
is indicated; city & school district election polling
places may differ.

WORD searching works best. WORDS can be any words
        included in a street name or zip code. City names,
        highway numbers, and section-township-range
        numbers are also considered to be WORDS.

        Enter W for WORD search
               S to   STOP or SWITCH to another Library
                       catalog

The information in this database is provided by the El
Paso County Clerk and Recorder; please refer questions
to Penrose Public Library: phone # (719) 531-6333,
extension 2254.

Type the letter for the kind of search you want and
press <RETURN>.
        SELECTED DATABASE: El Paso Legislative

ENTER COMMAND (?H FOR HELP) >> w

REMEMBER — WORDS are words included in a street name or
zip code. City names, highway numbers, and section-
township-range numbers are also WORDS.

For most searches enter BOTH a street and a zip code on
one line. It is best to exclude words such as STREET,
PLACE, COURT, etc.

For example, if your street is Astrozon Place in
Colorado Springs, zip code 80916, you should type (word
order is not important)
                ASTROZON 80916
        or   80916 ASTROZON
        or   ASTROZON COLORADO SPRINGS

Exhibit Y Continued

Numbered street names (1st, 2nd, etc.) should be
entered as if entirely spelled out (FIRST, SECOND,
etc.).

  For example: TWENTY SECOND 80904

Highway locations should be entered with the word
HIGHWAY and the number.
  For example: HIGHWAY 105 80133

Section-township-range (rural areas) should be entered
as numbers.
  For example: 08-13-60 80864

Enter words separated by spaces and press <RETURN>.

>union 80918

 WORKING . . .
UNION 53 ITEMS
UNION + 80918 19 ITEMS

For the 19 items that have
UNION + 80918
Press <RETURN>, or type <Q>UIT for a new search.

UNION + 80918 4 ITEMS

You may make your search more specific (and reduce the
size of the list) by adding another word to your
search. The result will be items in your current list
that also contain the new word.

to ADD a new word, enter it,

<D>ISPLAY to see the current list, or

<Q>UIT for a new search:

NEW WORD(S): d
1 Zip code 80918   PPLD
Street: union blvd n 4601-5099   VOTER INFORMATION
(odd numbers)

2 Zip code 80918   PPLD
Street: union blvd n 5100-5499   VOTER INFORMATION
(all numbers)

3 Zip code 80918   PPLD
Street: union blvd n 5500-5698   VOTER INFORMATION
(even numbers)

4 Zip code 80918   PPLD
Street: union blvd n 5501-5699   VOTER INFORMATION
(odd numbers)

<RETURN> TO CONTINUE DISPLAY

Exhibit Y Continued

ENTER <LINE NUMBER(S)> TO DISPLAY FULL RECORDS
<P>REVIOUS FOR PREVIOUS PAGE OR <Q>UIT FOR NEW
SEARCH 10

----------------------El Paso Legislative-------------
AUTHOR(s): ZIP CODE: 80918
TITLE(s):   STREET: UNION BLVD N 5500-5698 (EVEN NUMBERS)
                PRECINCT NUMBER 175
                SCHOOL DISTRICT 11
                U.S. CONGRESSIONAL DISTRICT 5
                STATE SENATE DISTRICT 9
                STATE REPRESENTATIVE DISTRICT 18
                COUNTY COMMISSIONER DISTRICT 1

                POLLING PLACE: VISTA GRANDE COMMUNITY
                            CHURCH 5440 N UNION BLVD
OTHER ENTRIES: GEOG AREA: COLORADO SPRINGS   80918
                DATE ENTERED:15-JUN-92
CALL #: VOTER INFORMATION   LIBRARY:
---3 of 4--------------------El Paso Legislative-------
<RETURN> to continue, <Q>UIT for a new search,
or <R>EPEAT this display, ? for HELP >

EXHIBIT Z

LOCAL GOVERNMENT

CITY HALL ON-LINE   OTHER GOVERNMENT
A joint project of the
City of Colorado Springs
and the Pikes   51. Local Documents (and
Peak Library District.   elected officials)
                                 52. El Paso County
                                     Legislative
44. News Releases   Districts (school,
45. City Council Agenda   congressional,
46. City Council Minutes   county)
47. City Source

Enter the NUMBER of your choice, and press the <RETURN>
key >>44 WORKING . . .

        SELECTED DATABASE: City News Releases

This database contains news releases issued by the
City of Colorado Springs during the most recent 30
days.

Exhibit Z Continued

You can search this database in two ways:

1. To search by SUBJECT, use the WORD search <W> command. All words contained in a news release are considered WORDS, including keywords from the title, subjects, and names of persons.

2. To see a list of the current news releases, in title order, use the QUICKSEARCH TITLE BROWSE command <//T%>.

```
Enter  W      for WORD search
       //T%   to  browse by TITLE
       S      to  STOP or SWITCH to another Library
              catalog
```

Type the letter for the kind of search you want and press <RETURN>.

SELECTED DATABASE: City News Releases

ENTER COMMAND (?H FOR HELP) >> w

REMEMBER — WORDS can be keywords from the title or can be subjects, city departments, geographic areas, events, or named individuals mentioned in the news release.

```
for example — subject          PARKS
              city department  DEPARTMENT OF UTILITIES
              geographic area  ROCKRIMMON
              event            SPRINGSPREE
              individual       BOB ISAAC
```

EXHIBIT AA

Enter word or words (no more than one line, please) separated by spaces and press <RETURN>.

```
>cable television

WORKING . . .
CABLE 1 ITEM
CABLE + TELEVISION 1 ITEM



1                                      PPLD —
   Cable tv advisory committee

Enter <LINE NUMBER> to display full record,
or <Q>UIT for new search
```

Exhibit AA Continued

```
----------------------City News Releases-------------
TITLE(s):        Cable TV Advisory Committee
     Terry McCann          4:30 p.m.; November 16, 1992
RELEASE AT WILL
```

Citizens of Colorado Springs having questions or concerns about Cable TV service in the city have an "ear" in the city administration. The Cable TV Advisory Committee was organized in August, 1991 to advise City Council about cable television service and programming in Colorado Springs. The committee also serves as a citizens' sounding board about local cable service, monitors trends in citizen concerns and works closely with the existing cable television company(ies) to resolve concerns and improve communications. Additionally, the committee makes service-change recommendations to the Council and monitors the compliance of agreements between the city and cable television companies.

If citizens have complaints regarding their Cablevision service, they should contact Colorado Springs Cablevision directly at 633-6616. If citizens have concerns regarding Cablevision issues in general, they should contact Mary Collins, City of Colorado Springs Municipal Operations Coordinator at 578-6600, who will relay this information to the committee.

This committee normally meets on the second Wednesday of each month at 4 p.m., at the City Administration Building, 30 S. Nevada Avenue.

```
---1 of 1------------------City News Releases---------
<RETURN> to continue, <Q>UIT for a new search,
or <R>EPEAT this display, ? for HELP >
You began with a WORD search on:
```

vide a timeless and placeless access to thousands of people who might not be able to easily enter through a library's doors. A movement in the direction of providing more and more online information resources available to anyone with a PC, modem, and a phone line has only resulted in even greater demand for the traditional books and other services available in our various library facilities. As we move ahead, we look for those important opportunities to expand our own local information network and, at the same time, to be part of the greater universe of library and information networks now bringing information to individual homes and businesses around the world. If it is indeed the same fire the melts the butter that hardens the egg, it also is the same desire for improved information access that will permit the virtual integration of thousands of information networks to create effortless access to information resources for anyone.

Project Mercury: The Virtual Library Infrastructure at Carnegie Mellon University

Barbara G. Richards
Associate University Librarian
Carnegie Mellon University
Pittsburgh, Pennsylvania

A dvances in information technologies are allowing increasing numbers of academic computing services to provide a campus network infrastructure with telecommunications links to an array of networked services. Faculty, students, and staff are using networks to access information that is not available locally. As observed in *Preferred Futures for Libraries*, "The *concept* [italics added] of the virtual library, i.e., a library that provides access to electronic and print materials from many sources, both local and remote has achieved a widespread popularity."[1] As a result librarians find themselves in a bewildering situation. The technology exists for libraries to provide reasonably easy access to a variety of electronic products and services. However, to design cost-effective library services that take advantage of these technologies and to manage and fund these services effectively is increasingly complex and difficult.

The current environment for university libraries can be characterized in part by an increase in the amount of information available combined with rising prices to acquire this information, increasing staff costs to manage library collections and services, and decreasing space to house these ever-burgeoning materials. These problem areas for libraries are compounded by the challenges facing universities as they strive toward quality in pursuing their educational mission. In order to increase their effectiveness and attract high-quality students in a shrinking student population, colleges and universities are placing renewed emphasis on undergraduate education. At the same time, universities are continuing vigorous research efforts to compete for fewer funding resources. Carnegie Mellon University and many other colleges and universities across the country are focused on defining the appropriate organizational structure to succeed and remain viable as quality institutions. In this environment a compelling argument for close collaboration between campus constituencies, particularly libraries and computing services, can be made. Universities must be able to effectively manage the wide variety of information resources required on campus in order to reduce redundancy of effort and to enhance the quality of the educational experience.

In 1986, library and computing administrators at Carnegie Mellon University began to discuss plans based on the idea that the electronic, or virtual, library was desired on campus. To develop building blocks for a virtual library, four critical areas needed to be addressed: (1) distributed storage and retrieval systems; (2) information capture and representation; (3) information retrieval and delivery; and (4) management and economics. Although Carnegie Mellon chose to focus initially on the first two critical areas, Project Mercury work will address each of these areas being faced by developers of virtual libraries. This chapter takes a look at one institution's work in the area of electronic, or virtual, libraries. Carnegie Mellon staff hopes that their experience in virtual libraries can be added to by many others, thereby advancing progress for the entire academic community.

Project Mercury Vision

In their article, "The Network is the Library," Mark Kibbey and Nancy Evans describe the ideal electronic library (which equates with today's virtual library terminology) as "a range of services and collections made accessible through networks." They contend that although there are several visions and various implementations of virtual libraries, they all have in common three characteristics: location independence, breadth of contents, and ease of use.[2] A virtual library embodying these characteristics could be successful in solving some important library management problems, particularly access to materials, collection size, and depth of coverage. Historically, the collections of libraries have always needed to be supplemented by accessing information not available on campus. The growth of collections did not keep pace with the growth of research activity on campus. Although great strides were made in enhancing collections during the late 1970s and early 1980s, it became clear that ownership of all required materials would never be feasible using current collection development methods.

At Carnegie Mellon the online public access catalog (OPAC) was released for campus use in 1984. In 1986, in response to growing demands for network access and additional electronic databases, the first library information system (LIS) was developed on an IBM 3083 using STAIRS as the database retrieval engine. The OPAC was just one of fourteen bibliographic and full-text databases. Access to library information was greatly facilitated by networked links to all areas of the campus. This mainframe system was popular, but retrieval was slow, the hardware was expensive and cumbersome to maintain, and it was difficult to add space for new databases. In addition, the interface used did not take advantage of the power of personal computers that were becoming widespread on campus. A new architecture was needed to begin to meet the increasing demands from campus users for a more powerful access and retrieval system.

In 1988 Carnegie Mellon University and the Online Computer Library Center (OCLC) formed Project Mercury to build a prototype of an electronic library. Major grants from the Pew Charitable Trusts and the Digital Equipment Corporation allowed the work to begin to build a second-generation library information system.[3] This prototype electronic library focused on providing a selection of information resources and services for the academic artificial intelligence community, including full-text documents (journal articles and technical reports) and bibliographic databases. As outlined in the first of a series of Mercury Technical Reports, the Mercury pilot design was based on three critical assumptions about the nature of information:

- Information should be stored at the most economically feasible location.
- Information should be a commodity wherever possible.
- Information should integrate with the workplace, regardless of workplace location.[4]

Having the content of library materials in electronic format and accessible over the network, in addition to merely using computing technologies to enhance library operations, was an idea that began to be articulated. This electronic library needed an affordable infrastructure with the capability of delivering all types of networked information, including full text, to desktop computers. The vision depicted scholars with personal computers retrieving information over the network and communicating with colleagues to share information, with the physical location of the scholars and the information being irrelevant. Once this infrastructure was established, the academic community's use of digital information and documents could be studied.

This new version of the LIS (or LIS II as it was called until the first version LIS was no longer in operation) was developed by the Project Mercury team, which included both library and computing staff. Releasing a large-scale distributed library on campus was an enormous undertaking, which took about two years and many hours of work for implementation. The LIS infrastructure, based on the concept of clients and servers linked through networked connections, allows for continued refinement and future development of this virtual library system.

Architecture

This distributed environment of clients and servers was implemented in the three university libraries' locations in October 1991 by the Project Mercury team. In January 1992, the system was in general use by the campus community. In May 1992, the IBM 3083 mainframe was decommissioned so that the new distributed LIS was the library system of record.

Figure 1 shows the general architecture of the current Carnegie Mellon University Library Information System as of August, 1994. The LIS architecture includes some important features necessary in the underlying structure of the virtual library, including security, design for multiple interfaces, multiple platforms that can be used, and the ability to access multiple types of documents.

The desktop clients are Unix workstations, Apple Macintoshes, and IBM PCs or compatibles and terminals. The client machines construct queries, send them to the servers, and provide an interactive display of information. Two interfaces are provided in the first release of the distributed LIS: a Motif user interface for Unix workstations running X.11 windows and a terminal interface for other machines. Until MAC and windows clients are developed, these clients must run the VT100 interface.

The server machines provide security, search and retrieval, and data manipulation such as sorting of titles. Databases are built on a DEC Alpha and moved to DECstation 5000 retrieval servers. Whenever possible, the LIS developers' strategy was to use software components already available, to incorporate existing or proposed standards, and to design the system to be machine independent. An extended Z39.50 version 1 is layered on TCP/IP to allow clients and servers to communicate. The database-building and retrieval software is Newton, developed by the Online Computer Library Center (OCLC).

Security for LIS is very important to users and vendors of commercial databases. In LIS this is accomplished by using an authentication system based on the Kerberos software, which was developed at Massachusetts

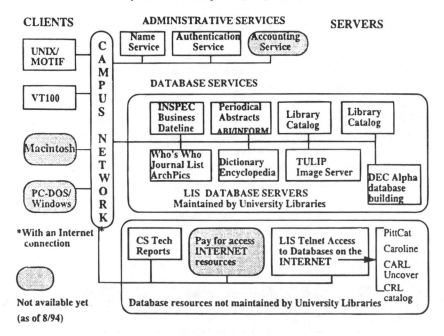

Figure 1. General system architecture as of August 1994

Institute of Technology. This software gives users the ability to log in to the campus network (Andrew) using a personal ID and password and to be authenticated to use all Andrew network resources. Once authenticated, valid Carnegie Mellon users may then use LIS, including the commercial databases licensed for use to Carnegie Mellon. It is not necessary to log in separately to LIS, once you have been validated.

The name service, currently implemented using the Andrew File System (AFS), functions to map database names to network addresses. In a distributed system it is relatively inexpensive to replicate databases for enhanced availability and performance. In the future the name service *could* provide the mechanism to select the least busy copy of the library catalog (which has two copies on two different servers), thereby splitting the usage load between servers by using redundant databases on different servers. This technique is used to improve the retrieval performance of the system. The library catalog currently gets about fifty percent of the use and the name service randomly selects a server for user log-in. The client-server architecture offers several advantages over the mainframe environment: the ability to split the load and balance maintenance, to increase the capacity of each server, and to scale upwards by adding new servers without having to disrupt the entire system.

Interface Design

The two interfaces that are currently available to LIS users are the Motif interface for Unix workstations running X.11 windows and the VT100 interface for all other machines. Some advantages of the Motif interface are that the user can open the three different window screens simultaneously, can easily move from one function or database to another, can see the results of searches and records retrieved at the same time, and can cut and paste information between window elements. Within machine limits, as much functionality as possible was built into the VT100 interfaces. Such functions as retaining the search history, printing, saving, and mailing records via the campus e-mail system are present for both interfaces. Figure 2, the Motif search window and Figure 3, the VT100 search window, are provided for comparison. The windowing capability of the Unix/Motif environment allows many enhancements to the search and display functionality that is not available with VT100. Figure 4 shows just one of the advanced features: the

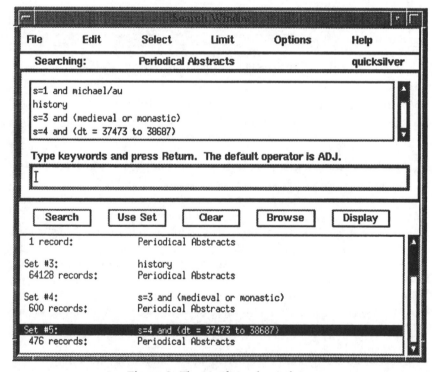

Figure 2. The Motif search window

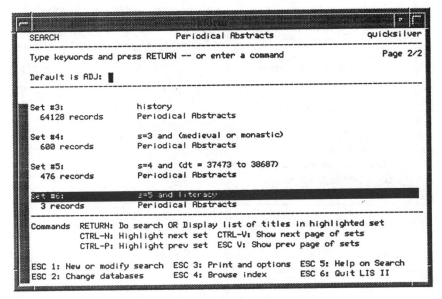

Figure 3. The VT100 search window

ability to open the search, browse, and record windows to view a total picture of the search session. The functionality exists to cut and paste between windows and to easily move between databases by "pointing and clicking" for selections on the pulldown menus.

From the start of the project, multiple interfaces were planned to make use of the personal computers and terminals that were already available to campus users. In the mainframe environment the power of a user's Unix workstation or personal computer was not utilized, but was required to act like a dumb terminal. With client-server architecture, the computing work is divided between the clients and the servers, making it possible for each particular machine type to have an interface that retains the "look and feel" of that particular machine. People who work on Unix workstations or Macintoshes are accustomed to a certain set of conventions that are used in designing the interfaces for applications on those machines, e.g., the native, user interface. The interface can be thought of as having two components: the framework and the data display within the framework. The framework varies according to the style of each machine type, while the display of data remains as consistent as possible among all interfaces. If these specific style conventions for particular machines are used in designing the LIS interface, then learning the way around an LIS screen interface becomes easier for users of particular machines. Also, with the native interface for different clients, the later integration of applications such as word processing, which run on those clients, is facilitated.

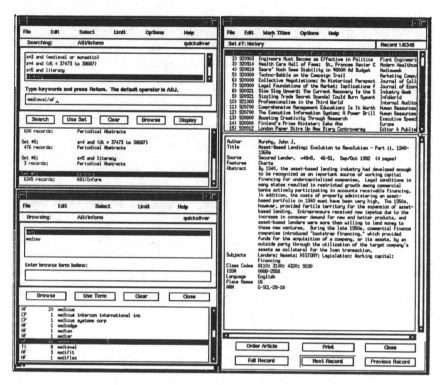

Figure 4. The Motif interface with the search, browse and record windows opened simultaneously

Designing an interface that would allow easy use of enhanced retrieval features requested by users, as well as make it usable by novices, continues to be a challenge. No topic engenders more discussion or is documented with more opinion than the design of these interfaces for LIS. Part of this is due to the fact that clients differ significantly in ways that affect user interface design—the amount of screen space; the capabilities of the client, e.g., the ability to display bit-mapped images; differences in vocabulary and procedures; and in the jargon and conventions of each client. Part of the issue is individual personal preference, usually based on which client is used most often. A great many tests were undertaken to design the interface, and these interface designs are under constant scrutiny. For more information on designing user interfaces see an article by Denise A. Troll.[5]

The second version of LIS is more complex to use because of its windowed environment and increased functionality. To provide users with guidance, online help is available from the menu and is accessible whenever needed. Each menu item interface must also be designed according to the appropriate style guide convention. Figure 5 (VT100) and Figure 6 (Motif) show examples of the Help table of contents that users view for the two interfaces. In addition to online help, printed manuals and guides to system use are available at all library locations.

The University Libraries have established an electronic bulletin board to specifically answer questions from users about LIS. Comments and questions can be sent from within the LIS search session. All questions are answered promptly by e-mail. The response is sent to the individual as well as the bulletin board.

Enhanced Retrieval Architecture

Carnegie Mellon University Libraries began to add database services as early as 1986. With the implementation of version two of the LIS with enhanced retrieval and display capabilities, the utility of the databases were increased. OCLC's Newton, optimized for large databases and Boolean retrieval, is the database building and retrieval software currently used in LIS. In the future, the system may also support other database search/retrieval software such as Ful/Text from Fulcrum, WAIS (Wide Area Information Server) from Thinking Machines or Mosaic for World Wide Web (WWW). The retrieval protocol is version one of Z39.50, called Z39.58. This protocol is a command language standard that specifies details such as the default search operator (adjacency). LIS users familiar with the default "and" operator in the first LIS had difficulty at the start with the "adj" default operator. However, a

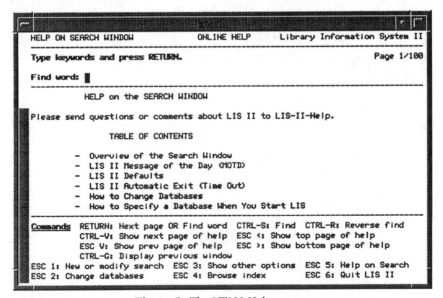

Figure 5. The VT100 Help screen

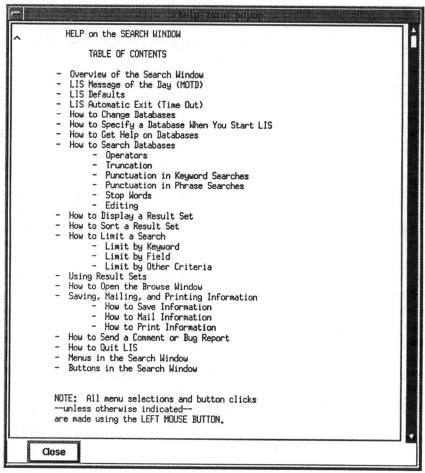

Figure 6. The Motif Help window

search result of "zero hits" automatically gives the user the opportunity to redo a search using the "and" operator. This help, plus the fact that writing to an agreed-upon standard will make it possible to send queries to other servers using the same retrieval protocols at other sites, is making acceptance somewhat easier to obtain. Users are anxious to be able to search other university catalogs using an interface that they have already learned.

Electronic Resources

The LIS contains a collection of campus and commercial databases in two formats: ASCII and bit-mapped page images. Commercial bibliographic databases were chosen for inclusion based on whether they improved bibliographic access to the local collection or to subject areas where greater access is required. Two databases with possible links to full-text documents were chosen for experimentation in the areas of timely delivery of information, storage costs, and the cost of owning versus accessing library materials. As of August, 1994, LIS contained the following ASCII databases:

Local Campus Information Databases

Library catalog. A bibliographic database representing approximately 800,000 items (books, films, sound recordings, software, scores, etc.) in the Carnegie Mellon University Libraries. The MARC records for these holdings are being enhanced in several ways by library staff to study the effect on retrieval. Library cataloging staff members add author-supplied abstracts to records for computer science technical reports, both for those produced at Carnegie Mellon and at the approximately 200 other institutions whose reports we collect. They also key in tables of contents to the 505 field of MARC records for books with individually authored chapters and other specified table of contents under current guidelines.[6]

Journal list. A database of Carnegie Mellon University Libraries' periodical holdings, particularly current and noncurrent journals, but also some monographic series. The journal list contains summary holdings (e.g., v. 1, 1960-present). More detailed holdings and complete information on serial title changes may be found in the library catalog database.

ArchPics. A database, maintained by staff in Fine Arts, that indexes pictures and drawings of over 3,000 modern buildings selected from books in the University Libraries' collection.

Who's who at Carnegie Mellon. A database of faculty, students, and staff at Carnegie Mellon, that contains names, addresses, telephone numbers, and department affiliations.

Research directory. Provides information on faculty and their research interests in each of Carnegie Mellon University's undergraduate academic departments, graduate schools, research institutes, and research centers. Published annually.

Commercial Information Databases

ABI/INFORM, 1986–present (UMI). Bibliographic records with abstracts that index over 750 periodical publications covering business, management, and company information.

INSPEC (Information Services for Physics, Electronics and Computing), 1988–present (IEEE). Bibliographic records with abstracts that index scholarly publications in communications, computing, electrical engineering, electronics, physics, and information technology.

Materials Science, 1992, (Elsevier Science). Bibliographic records with abstracts for articles in forty-three scholarly research publications in fields of metals, alloys, semiconductor materials, ceramics, polymers, composites, materials analysis, and related areas. Records in this database are linked to the page images in the TULIP image database.

Newspaper Abstracts, 1989–present (UMI). Bibliographic records with abstracts for articles from eight major newspapers, including the *New York Times, Wall Street Journal, Washington Post*, and others.

Periodical Abstracts, 1986–present (UMI). Bibliographic records with abstracts to articles in over 1,000 general and scholarly journals and magazines in the social sciences, arts, humanities, general sciences, and current affairs.

Full-text Databases of Commercial Information (ASCII format)

Academic American Encyclopedia (Grolier). A full text encyclopedia.

American Heritage Dictionary (Houghton-Mifflin). A full text dictionary that includes synonyms.

Business Dateline, 1992–present (UMI). A full-text database containing articles from 180 regional business publications from across the country, including monthly magazines, weekly tabloids, and daily newspapers.

Although the LIS now has the technical infrastructure to begin adding more databases, outstanding questions remain about the direction for locally mounted databases. The answer to the questions of what electronic materials should be locally owned and what can be accessed over networks has considerable impact on the local collection of materials. The environment becomes increasingly complex as decisions are made for the purchase or lease of electronic materials. Subscriptions to tape products are expensive. But this is not the total cost of providing the material. Costs beyond the subscription price for the tape or CD-ROM need to be considered, that is, for technical support and additional equipment. How to allocate acquisitions funds for electronic materials becomes a larger question in these times of rising costs and static or declining acquisitions budgets. The balance between print and electronic collections is a complex issue, which we must begin to address in a systematic way.

Electronic materials need additional technical support beyond what other formats have required. At present no vendor can supply tapes that can be loaded without several months of programming work to index and load the tapes for the Newton search and retrieval software. As the number of years of tape data for our current subscriptions grows, decisions need to be made about the number of years of back files to be kept active online. Budgets for materials as well as capital purchase of equipment need to be made simultaneously. Information about the use of electronic products is very much needed to plan the direction for the future.

In May, 1994, a new version of LIS software was released to campus that allows the user to search databases at sites other than Carnegie Mellon that do not currently charge a licensing or search fee. If the user selects a menu item "Databases not at CMU", a telnet window is opened and the user is connected to the database using the campus Internet connection. However, the search protocol used is the one provided by the maintainer of the database. Currently four databases may be accessed from this menu: *PittCat*, the library catalog of the University of Pittsburgh providing access to more than one million titles; *Caroline*, the library catalog of the Carnegie Library of Pittsburgh with about 700,000 book titles indexed; *CARL UnCover*, a table of contents database indexing more than 15,000 journals in a wide variety of subject areas and The Center for Research Libraries (CRL) catalog with records for more than 350,000 items. Located in Chicago, Illinois the CRL collects and houses research materials of many types.

Carnegie Mellon has also implemented a CD-ROM network within the three university libraries' sites that is not linked with the campus network. For databases with less use, this network may prove satisfactory—if users can ultimately connect to it thorough the LIS. The libraries have a very long list of suggested new databases, both commercial and local, that may make good additions to LIS. This "wish list" has been carefully prioritized based on librarians' selection criteria that will enhance the libraries' ability to deliver information services. With an increasing number of options for accessing databases through the LIS without loading them locally, the choice of the most cost-effective option is complicated. Again, striking the balance between various alternatives for access to commercial databases and local mounting of high-use commercial and local information databases that are not available elsewhere is critical to cost and ease of user access.

Information retrieval would be enhanced if the capability of linking databases were present in LIS. Several projects that focus on the linking of databases for the purposes of retrieval or document delivery have not yet been started. Preliminary work on building these links has shown it will require more time than originally predicted in early 1992. In the future we hope to add links from catalog records to records in the *Current Reviews for College Libraries* (*Choice*). This would be an additional enhancement to catalog records making the users' selection of relevant library items more precise. Links from bibliographic databases, such as INSPEC, which allow users to know whether a journal is in the library collection in either print or electronic format, is highly desired. Links from the circulation records in the library management system to LIS, that allow users to know whether an item is available, is also high on users' lists of additions to LIS. These projects will be done when time and funding resources permit.

Image Projects

Two projects are currently in progress that utilize software to display bit-mapped images on the user's screen. The records in bibliographic databases are linked to full-text databases in bit-mapped page image format to provide document delivery. These projects with different partners are experiments to study use of this format of electronic information by the campus community. Each of the current projects is designed to address a different range of users and questions.

The initial project, done in collaboration with several publishers, to develop image display and network transmission software was completed in December, 1992. This project marked a significant step forward in the ability to handle image databases by the development of software to deliver bit-mapped images across the campus network, linking the images to a bibliographic database, and providing an image browser for viewing the pages. Elsevier Science, the American Association for Artificial Intelligence (AAAI) and the Institute of Electrical and Electronics Engineers (IEEE) gave permission to scan articles from seven academic journals in the fields of computer science, artificial intelligence and electrical and electronics engineering. Approximately 31,000 pages were scanned from *Artificial Intelligence, Cognition, IEEE Computer, Journal of Logic Programming, Parallel Computing, Science of Computer Programming and Theoretical Computer Science*. The scanner used was a DEC MD400 (RICOH IS 50) that averages four pages per minute at 400 dpi. Uncompressed, each page image is approximately 1.7MB. Using TIFF Group 4 Fax compression, the compressed size is approximately 60K. The compressed images are stored on the retrieval server in hierarchical directories by journal name, volume, and number. They are sent across the network at the user's request and decompressed and displayed for the client as the image arrives. Currently only Unix clients (DECstations and Sun Sparcstations) have the ability to display these images. In the future, Macintosh and DOS with windows clients will be developed to allow image display.

This project developed mechanisms to make images available in two ways: linked to records in a bibliographic database and through a document browser. In this case the test database of scanned images was linked to bibliographic records in INSPEC. If users are searching the INSPEC database and a full-text image is available for the article citation received, an image button becomes active to allow screen viewing of the article. When the document image is on the screen, the image software allows navigation through the pages of the article, which is similar to leafing through the pages of a journal, starting with the table of contents. This test database, with the associated software to provide bit-mapped images linked to a bibliographic database and image browser, demonstrated the feasibility of this type of document delivery across the campus network. It became clear as the project progressed that the production scanning which was necessary to build, maintain and keep current such a database was not sustainable by library staff. However, the software developed in this project is now being used in the two current image linking projects with University Microfilms (UMI) and Elsevier Science in the TULIP project.

The project with University Microfilms Inc. (UMI) is designed to link two bibliographic databases (*Periodical Abstracts* and *ABI/INFORM*) to the full-text bit-mapped page images supplied by UMI on CD-ROM. These bibliographic records in the databases mounted in the LIS contain article reference numbers (ARNs) that identify where the full-text page images of the articles can be found on the corresponding CD-ROM product, *General Periodicals Ondisc* or *Business Periodicals Ondisc*. The CD-ROM jukeboxes are located in a room in the main library. In Phase I of this pilot project, called E-JADS, users can submit requests for articles using an ordering screen that activates when users are searching in either of the two bibliographic databases on LIS. The order request sends e-mail to a library employee who prints the articles on a laser printer. The libraries currently operate a manual Journal Article Delivery Service (JADS) in which articles are copied from journals in the Carnegie Mellon collection and are delivered by campus mail to the Carnegie Mellon user community for a nominal fee. Fees for the E-JADS service will be the same as those charged for the articles delivered through JADS. The ultimate objective is to provide the user with the ability to view articles on the workstations and then to be able to print them on a local printer, depending on the utility of the article, the availability of suitable printing facilities and adherence to any copyright restrictions on the information. Figure 7 shows the announcement dialog box for the E-JADS service, and Figure 8 shows the order screen for obtaining the printed article.

The second project, TULIP (The Universities LIcensing Program), is a collaborative project between Elsevier Scientific Publishers and participants from fifteen universities. Each university is working on some aspect of the problem of handling electronic journals in projects that address these broad categories: technical, organizational, economic, and user behavior. Elsevier

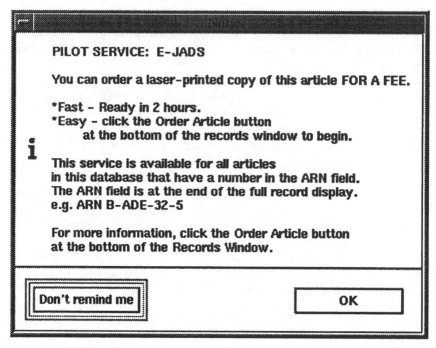

Figure 7. The E-JADS Pilot Service announcement dialog box

Scientific Publishers are providing the participants with a page-image database of forty-three journals in the field of materials science and engineering. With this number of participants, it is hoped that the results of the combined experimental projects will lead to findings that will contribute to understanding how to accelerate the distribution of journal material in electronic format. Elsevier plans to report progress in an irregular newsletter, *TULIP The Universities Licensing Program*, which was first issued in November 1992.

As described in the first TULIP newsletter, these journals will be provided in the following files: TIFF bit-mapped page images (cover to cover, including table of contents) scanned from the printed page at 300 dpi, Group 4 fax compression; edited and structured ASCII "heads" for each editorial item, including bibliographic citations and article abstract; and unedited OCR (Optical Character Recognition)-generated ASCII full text (for searching, not display). The files will be provided biweekly. For 1992, these journals will publish 103,000 pages and will require 11GB of storage. Elsevier will create the files and ship them to Engineering Information (EI), which will maintain the archive and act as Internet host. EI will redistribute or otherwise provide access over the Internet to the updates. Each university will receive according to each university profile and, receive without charge dur-

```
┌─────────────────────────────────────────────────────────────┐
│ ▄▄▄▄▄▄▄▄▄▄▄▄▄▄▄▄▄▄▄▄▄▄▄▄▄▄▄▄▄▄▄▄▄▄▄▄▄▄▄▄▄▄▄▄▄▄▄▄▄▄▄▄▄▄▄▄▄▄▄▄ │
│                        PRINT ARTICLE                         │
│  Your Name or UserID:  ┌────────────────────────────────┐    │
│                        │ hamlet▌                        │    │
│                        └────────────────────────────────┘    │
│  ──────────────────────────────────────────────────────────  │
│  Select one method of PAYMENT:                               │
│  ◇  Pay by Copicard (purchase at Circulation Desk.)          │
│          Present Copicard at time of pickup.                 │
│  ◇  Charge to my CMU or JADS (Journal Article Delivery Service)│
│          account number. Enter number:      ┌───────────┐    │
│                                             └───────────┘    │
│  ──────────────────────────────────────────────────────────  │
│  Allow 2 hours for printing.                                 │
│  Select one method of DELIVERY:                             │
│  ◇   Pickup articles at the Periodicals Office, 3rd Floor, Hunt Library.│
│          See Help for service hours.                        │
│  ◇  Deliver in campus mail (CMU or JADS account payments only).│
│          Enter campus address:              ┌───────────┐    │
│                                             └───────────┘    │
│  REMEMBER, the article you want may be available AT NO CHARGE │
│  if CMU has a print or microform subscription. See Help for details.│
│  DISCLAIMER:                                                 │
│  When necessary, we will issue reprints but not refunds. Articles│
│  may NOT be returned because content is not as expected. However,│
│  users will not be charged for errors in the database (i.e. improperly│
│  scanned articles, etc.).                                   │
│  ┌──────────────────┐   ┌────────────┐   ┌────────┐         │
│  │  PRINT ARTICLE   │   │   CANCEL   │   │  HELP  │         │
│  └──────────────────┘   └────────────┘   └────────┘         │
└─────────────────────────────────────────────────────────────┘
```

Figure 8. The E-JADS print article order form

ing the project, the electronic full text (bit-mapped and ASCII) for those journals that they subscribe to in paper. They will also receive the bibliographic information for all forty-three journals and will have on-demand access on a pay-per-use model to those titles to which they do not subscribe.[7]

Carnegie Mellon plans to provide broad campus access to the bit-mapped images through the image software that has been developed for LIS. Carnegie Mellon has a sizable population of faculty, students (undergraduates and graduates), and researchers working in the field of materials science engineering or closely related fields. This project is very important to increase understanding of networked delivery and use of electronic journals. Having a critical mass of images in a subject area will allow the gathering of both usage and user behavior data.

Currently LIS delivers full-text electronic documents in ASCII format from the *Academic American Encyclopedia* and *Business Dateline*. A third method of delivery being tested in the projects described is that of bit-mapped page image. Images in the test database are deliverable to the workstation. The image window provides multiple levels of "zoom" so that text is easily legible for online viewing. Figure 9 shows an image document as it appears on the screen. Figure 10 provides several more levels of "zoom in" to show greater detail in the document.

As we develop a critical mass of images available to users, work is progressing on the technically difficult task of releasing the image software to the entire campus through LIS. All of the above described projects have some common characteristics. They are all pilot projects of an experimental nature that will extend our understanding of alternative methods of document delivery and allow one to study user behavior in relation to the use of electronic materials, especially materials in bit-mapped page image format. The provision of full-text and image databases enhances retrieval, and some measure of user satisfaction will be determined by how well document delivery is linked with this retrieval.

The document delivery goals are twofold: to facilitate the delivery of printed documents to the user's local printer (whether in offices, library sites, clusters, and dorms) and the delivery of electronic documents to the user's desktop. Delivery of printed documents will be facilitated by having online requesting capability for such services as courier/interlibrary loan, in which physical articles in the local or remote site are delivered to a campus location; print, in which full text of articles are delivered from an electronic resource; materials check-out, in which the requested item in the local collection is checked out to the user and is held for pick-up or delivered; and materials reserve, by which faculty can place orders for items to be placed in physical or electronic reserve locations. As electronic documents become more prevalent, new ways of dealing with access and delivery will need to be explored.

Statements suggesting that technological changes have the potential for fundamentally transforming library operations are beginning to have an impact on the way librarians view the building of virtual libraries. The many experimental projects currently in progress and reported on at each task force meeting of the Coalition for Networked Information will have far reaching effects on library operations and services.[8] In a practical treatise, *Redesigning Library Services: A Manifesto,* Michael Buckland states that library services have existed for years to provide access to documents, to support the mission of the institution, and to support the interests of the populations served. Buckland makes a strong case that current trends in information technology mandate that library services be examined and redesigned in light of the utility of the opportunities that are presented. No one knows exactly how libraries will be transformed, but there is no doubt that they will be.[9]

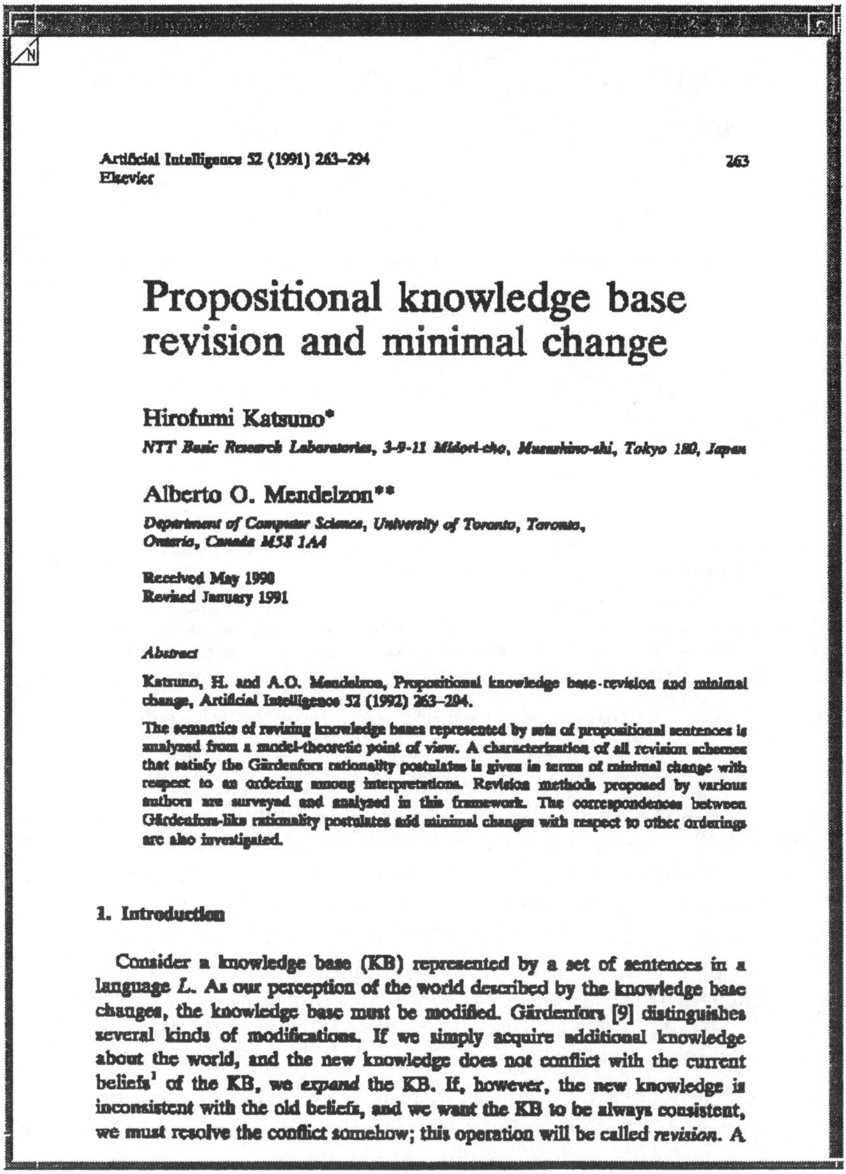

Artificial Intelligence 52 (1991) 263–294
Elsevier

263

Propositional knowledge base revision and minimal change

Hirofumi Katsuno*
NTT Basic Research Laboratories, 3-9-11 Midori-cho, Musashino-shi, Tokyo 180, Japan

Alberto O. Mendelzon**
Department of Computer Science, University of Toronto, Toronto, Ontario, Canada M5S 1A4

Received May 1990
Revised January 1991

Abstract

Katsuno, H. and A.O. Mendelzon, Propositional knowledge base revision and minimal change, Artificial Intelligence 52 (1992) 263–294.

The semantics of revising knowledge bases represented by sets of propositional sentences is analyzed from a model-theoretic point of view. A characterization of all revision schemes that satisfy the Gärdenfors rationality postulates is given in terms of minimal change with respect to an ordering among interpretations. Revision methods proposed by various authors are surveyed and analyzed in this framework. The correspondences between Gärdenfors-like rationality postulates and minimal changes with respect to other orderings are also investigated.

1. Introduction

Consider a knowledge base (KB) represented by a set of sentences in a language L. As our perception of the world described by the knowledge base changes, the knowledge base must be modified. Gärdenfors [9] distinguishes several kinds of modifications. If we simply acquire additional knowledge about the world, and the new knowledge does not conflict with the current beliefs[1] of the KB, we expand the KB. If, however, the new knowledge is inconsistent with the old beliefs, and we want the KB to be always consistent, we must resolve the conflict somehow; this operation will be called *revision*. A

Figure 9. The image document as it appears on the screen of a Unix workstation

Current library administration and organization has been primarily designed for print resources. A compelling case can be made for the transformational nature of digital technologies if one looks at the transformations that took place over centuries as the world's people went from an oral tradition of communication to a print culture and now into digital technolo-

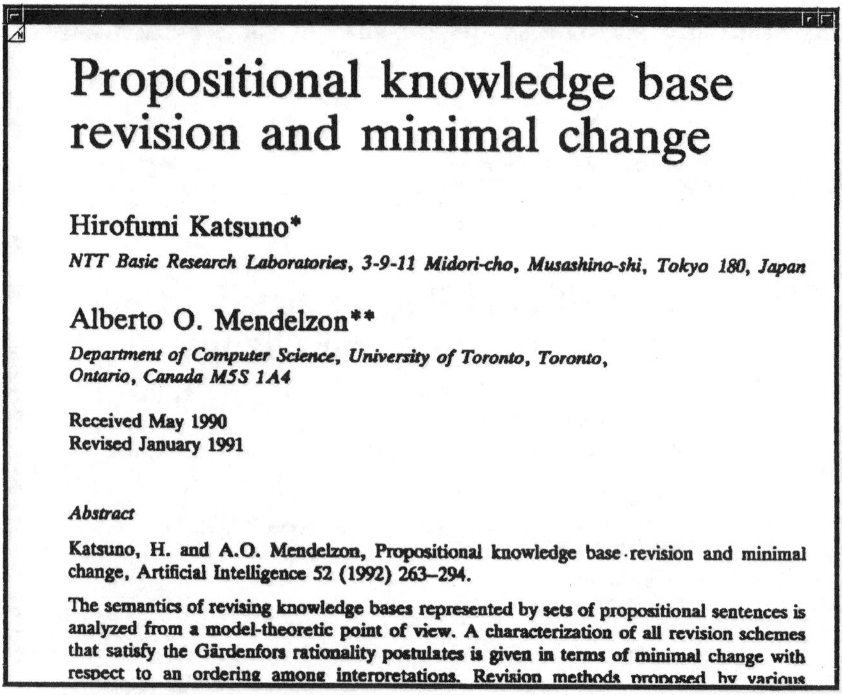

Propositional knowledge base revision and minimal change

Hirofumi Katsuno*

NTT Basic Research Laboratories, 3-9-11 Midori-cho, Musashino-shi, Tokyo 180, Japan

Alberto O. Mendelzon**

Department of Computer Science, University of Toronto, Toronto, Ontario, Canada M5S 1A4

Received May 1990
Revised January 1991

Abstract

Katsuno, H. and A.O. Mendelzon, Propositional knowledge base revision and minimal change, Artificial Intelligence 52 (1992) 263–294.

The semantics of revising knowledge bases represented by sets of propositional sentences is analyzed from a model-theoretic point of view. A characterization of all revision schemes that satisfy the Gärdenfors rationality postulates is given in terms of minimal change with respect to an ordering among interpretations. Revision methods proposed by various

Figure 10. An image with the "zoom" feature used to enlarge the type

gies. Far-reaching changes have come each time, but they were not known in advance. Who would have predicted the democratization of information as a result of the printing press? For the foreseeable future, we will have print, digital, and multimedia formats to service. What sort of transformations will happen when library services must not only contain electronic materials but the services themselves are supplied by electronic means? What happens when print is not the predominate form of the material? How do we get through the transition? These questions remain to be answered as we continue our work with virtual libraries.

The currently implemented architecture for the LIS is a good beginning for demonstrating the potential to transform library services. The computer hardware and software have already been used to enhance present library services. Using a distributed model of computing, the way information is collected, organized, stored, preserved, retrieved, and disseminated can be fundamentally changed. In this process, the technology will also change the way in which the Carnegie Mellon University Libraries support the university's mission in education, research and transfer of technology.

The current practice of interlibrary loan is a good example of where radical transformations are ready to take place. In the past, each individual campus tried to collect those materials that would enable individuals to pursue their scholarly activities to a large extent within the confines of the campus community. This led to very sizable collections at research institutions. The quality of the collections was judged primarily on the depth and breadth in various subject areas. Managing these large collections for access to and preservation of the information continues to be an enormous, and vital, library service. The widespread growth of OPACs beginning in the mid-1980s is testimony to the fact that having digital descriptive records in an online public access catalog with a keyword or Boolean retrieval system is an extremely useful access tool.

During this time there was also rapid growth of networks, especially for the scholarly and research community. Interlibrary loan, a longstanding arrangement between libraries to get materials for their constituents, is clearly based on moving physical items, usually print, but other materials as well. What is happening with the rise of networks and electronic libraries? Those libraries that have tried to maximize access to materials and optimize resources used to purchase items have begun to see that material in digital format might offer another increment in efficiency. This can, and is, happening now that infrastructures using digital technologies are in place. It is possible to construct many alternative scenarios for Interlibrary Loan activity.

The implementation of the virtual library has set the stage for change and redesign in the way we access and use resources other than our local collections. What will be the nature of this redesign? How will all the current players in the information arena be aligned with one another? Only as we continue to be partners in the solution will we find answers that will benefit the information community as a whole.

Endnotes

1. Dougherty, Richard M., and Carol Hughes. *Preferred Futures for Libraries: A Summary of Six Workshops with University Provosts and Library Directors.* Mountain View, CA: The Research Libraries Group, 1991. p. 4.

2. Evans, Nancy H., and Mark H. Kibbey "The Network is the Library." *EDUCOM Review* (Fall 1989): 15–20.

3. Project Mercury and the University Libraries gratefully acknowledge support from The Pew Charitable Trusts, Digital Equipment Corporation, American Association for Artificial Intelligence (AAAI), Online Computer Library Center (OCLC), Apple Computer, Bell Atlantic, Institute of Electrical and Electronics Engineers (IEEE), and Elsevier Science Publishers.

4. Evans, Nancy H., Denise A. Troll, Mark H. Kibbey, Thomas J. Michalak, and William Y. Arms. "The Vision of the Electronic Library." Mercury Technical Report Series, Number 1. Pittsburgh: Carnegie Mellon University, 1989.

5. Troll, Denise A. "Designing the Gateway Interface: Tips and Techniques from Carnegie Mellon's Experience." In *Emerging Communities: Integrating Networked Information into Library Services.* Ann Bishop, ed. Urbana-Champaign: University of Illinois, 1994. 101–119. (Papers presented at the 1993 Clinic on Library Applications of Data Processing, April 4–6, 1993.)

6. For details about enhanced catalog record processing see Michalak, Thomas J. "An experiment in enhancing catalog records at Carnegie Mellon University." *Library Hi Tech* v. 31, 3 (1990): 33–41.

7. Additional details may be found in *TULIP The Universities Licensing Program,* Number 1 (Nov. 1992). New York: Elsevier Science Publishers, 1992.

8. One example is Charles Henry and Paul Evan Peters. "The Transformational Potential of Networked Information: An Overview of the Theme for the Fall 1992 Meeting of the Task Force of the Coalition for Networked Information." October 29, 1992.

9. Michael Buckland. *Redesigning Library Services: A Manifesto.* Chicago: ALA, 1992.

The Internet at Arizona State University:A Case Study in Networking

George S. Machovec
Technical Coordinator
Colorado Alliance of Research Libraries
Denver, Colorado
formerly Head, Library Technology and Systems
Arizona State University

A rizona State University (ASU) is an emerging research institution on two campuses—the ASU Main campus has 40,000 students and the ASU West campus has 5,000 students. ASU employs over 1,500 faculty and 5,000 support staff. ASU accesses the worldwide Internet through a regional network called WESTNET, which covers Utah, Arizona, and New Mexico. Two major Internet nodes are in Arizona, one at the University of Arizona (Tucson) and the second at ASU (Tempe). All Internet connections in southern Arizona go through the University of Arizona while all institutions in central and northern Arizona have access through Arizona State University. In this regard, ASU has taken a leadership role in offering wide-scale access to this national information highway.

Growth

In August 1988, ASU had one outgoing terminal server and one connection on its Academic VAX to WESTNET. By 1991, all of the campus mainframes, the library's Tandem/CARL system, and over eighty departmental Banyan, Novell, AppleTalk and DECNET LANs were connected to the Ethernet. Users on these hosts have varying levels of access to the Internet, and there are also over 2,000 direct-connected microcomputers to this campus network.

In addition to the on-campus users, ASU has become a regional node to all institutions and individuals in central and northern Arizona requiring access to the Internet. This includes users in Maricopa County such as ASU West, the Arizona Board of Regents, ASU Downtown Center, Grand Canyon University, the Maricopa County Community College District (MCCCD), American Graduate School for International Management, Intel, Honeywell Bull, and others. In addition, organizations such as Northern Arizona University (Flagstaff) and Embry-Riddle (Prescott) also connect through the ASU node (see Figure 1).

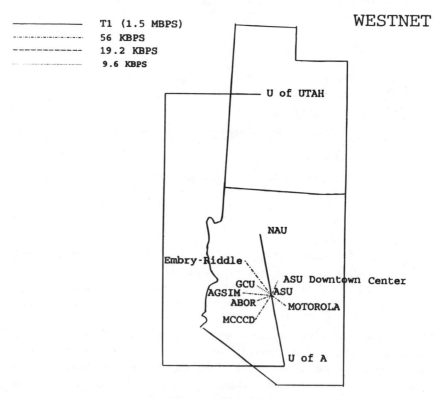

Figure 1. WESTNET map

A number of public libraries in Arizona have connected or are in the process of connecting, to the Internet through ASU. These include Phoenix Public Library, Scottsdale Public Library, and the Maricopa County Library District. What is particularly interesting with the public libraries is that they are acting as the catalyst for not only gaining connectivity for themselves but are also propelling their own municipal or county data processing centers into participating in this national network. Other public libraries have also expressed an interest, and it is expected that others will join in the next few years.

Connecting to the Internet Through ASU

For purposes of connecting to the network, there are a number of different levels that may be defined: personal and institutional. Once access is acquired, the full range of services are available, including online interactive sessions using telnet, file transfers (with ftp), and e-mail.

Individuals may gain access to the Internet at ASU by following several steps:

- ASU acts as a local dial-in node whereby individuals with microcomputers may call one of the local mini-frame or mainframe computers connected to the Internet or may gain access using the serial line interface protocol (SLIP).
- The caller must have an account on a campus computer to gain access to the network. In this way, Internet users from ASU are "good citizens" and may be tracked if problems develop.
- The user must pay for a campus computer account (if not affiliated with the university).

Institutional access may follow the above procedures, if higher levels of service are required the following steps are necessary:

- A class A, B, or C license for WESTNET may be acquired that will supply a range of IP (Internet Protocol) addresses to the organization to assign to its users.
- If the organization wants a dedicated leased line for its access, it must pay for its share of connectivity and all costs associated with connecting. This may include leased line charges, routers for both the local and ASU side, CSU/DSUs and other hardware that may be necessary for connectivity, and any infrastructure costs for Ethernet compatibility on the new user side.

In order for any institution to connect to the Internet through ASU the following procedures are necessary:

- Complete the "Making a Connection to WESTNET" form and return it to the ASU Telecommunications Services.

- Order the appropriate digital (DDS) circuit to extend from end-user site to ASU.

- Provide a letter of agency to the DDS circuit carrier to allow ASU Telecommunications Services or WESTNET NOC (Network Operations Center) staffs to troubleshoot the line when the end-user is not able.

- Provide an open serial port on a Cisco (or Cisco-compatible) router at the end-user location.

- Provide payment of $1,950 (one-time cost) to ASU Telecommunications Services for a serial interface in the ASU Cisco router.

- Provide a pair of 56KB CSU/DSUs (or other speed if necessary) for the DDS circuit. If the user acquires the ASU recommended brand, then ASU will provide backup equipment. Otherwise, the end-user must provide his/her own backup equipment.

- The user must make his/her own arrangements for connecting the new circuit into his/her own local network or computing environment.

ASU Libraries Internet Uses

The University Libraries at Arizona State University are using the Internet in a number of creative ways. As a point of reference, the University Libraries have approximately 3 million volumes, is ranked twenty-sixth in the Association of Research Libraries (ARL), and has a book budget of about $6 million dollars (including the ASU Main campus, ASU West and ASU Law Library). The library operates a Tandem CLX 860 computer with over 25GB of hard-disk storage, runs the CARL Systems software, operates over 500 terminals (or PCs), and runs a jointly shared system with ASU Main campus, ASU West campus, ASU Law Library, Northern Arizona University, and the American Graduate School for International Management. The CARL system at ASU supports over thirty databases and gateways.

Through the CARL system at ASU, transparent connectivity is provided to patrons for such systems as MELVYL (University of California), the Maricopa County Community Colleges system (a DRA system that runs ten community colleges in the Phoenix metropolitan area), and Phoenix Public Library (a CLSI system). Users merely select a category from the PAC screen, which indicates "Arizona Libraries" or "Out of State Libraries," and they are presented with a choice of remote library systems with which to connect. Once a selection is made, the user is automatically connected to the remote system. If it is a non-CARL system, the user must enter commands in the native protocol of that system. This can sometimes be a challenge for not only the patron but also reference librarians because it is not always immediately obvious where one is in the network, especially if a terminal is approached after another user has left it hanging in some unknown location (it will time back, but this may not occur before another person gets online).

ASU Libraries also use the Internet to run production staff and PAC terminals at the American Graduate School for International Management (AGSIM). AGSIM runs about a dozen staff (circulation, maintenance) and public access catalog (PAC) terminals in its library, which is located about thirty-five miles from the ASU Main campus. Originally a separate leased line was going to be acquired for operating these terminals, but it was soon realized that the 56KB Internet link for AGSIM was not being used to capacity, and it made financial sense to run the library terminals through this circuit. The big issue in this situation was security because it was realized that the Internet is inherently an open and unsecured environment.

Security for these production OPAC terminals was handled as follows:

- All in-library terminals were run through a Cisco router that only passed traffic from AGSIM. All other users are turned away.
- Once gaining access to a CARL staff menu, the user must supply a password to get off the screen.
- Once the staff menu screen is passed, the user is asked for a second-level password that provides access to the application.

Through the proper use of routing and double passwording, a reasonable level of security was provided. Although more sophisticated techniques of encryption or security access cards could be implemented, it was felt that this was an unneeded expense for the application. The system has been operational for over a year with no known breaches in security.

The ASU Libraries' PAC, CARL, has been available on the Internet since 1989. The system is not passworded at the system level for PAC, but user validation is required for access to specific databases (such as H. W. Wilson periodical indexes and the *Grolier's Academic American Encyclopedia*).

Every librarian in the University Libraries (over ninety) has a microcomputer and is connected to the campus network. Each is required to use the campus mail (IBM's Office Vision) and calender system. Many take advantage of the full range of Internet features such as e-mail, file transfers (using ftp), telnet access to remote information systems, listservs and USENET. Subject specialists in the library incorporate information about network access into the classes in their disciplines because many students have Internet access from computing sites on campus (i.e., rooms full of networked microcomputers), from mainframe accounts, via dial-in from home or through the library CARL interface.

Virtual Library Opportunities

The virtual library may be defined as a system by which a user may transparently connect to remote sources of relevant information specifically intended for his/her own study, research, teaching, or recreation. In order to take advantage of a number of opportunities in this area, the University Libraries at ASU has established a Virtual Library Demonstration Project in which librarians, faculty, and experts from Information Technology (i.e., the computer center) may jointly explore and develop cutting edge projects and products. As of spring 1993, a number of special projects have been envisioned and are in development including some advanced front-end products to run on MS-DOS, Macintosh and Unix clients, such as wide area information servers (WAIS), gophers, and other Internet navigational tools.

The site will not only be a testing ground for development work and navigational tools, but as products or services are brought to a more mature state, they may be put in production around campus. This will ensure that advanced development work will not only continue but that the virtual library project is not to be just a place but a staging ground for the general release of products and services that may be used anywhere, regardless of location.

Phoenix Metro Image Project

In October 1992, Arizona State University, the Maricopa County Community Colleges, and the Phoenix Public Library received a three-year Department of Education Title II-D networking grant for $371,000 ($271,000 will be received the first year). The project's goals were threefold:

- To provide access to ABI/INFORM from University Microfilms Incorporated (UMI) at Arizona State University on the CARL System for consortium use.

- To establish an Internet link between Arizona State University and Phoenix Public Library (the link already exists for Maricopa County Community Colleges).

- To develop and evaluate a Unix-based request server to enable the automated transmission of imaged articles in response to requests by users.

A unique feature of this grant is that ABI/INFORM will be loaded at ASU and then networked to all three library systems, all operating with different OPACs (online public access catalogs). This will offer several advantages: the file will be loaded one time to be made available to users on all three systems (CARL, DRA, and CLSI), greater computer literacy for patrons will be developed as users move between systems, consortium pricing can be acquired for initial and ongoing licensing fees from UMI, ongoing processing will need to be done at one computer site, and distributed dial-in nodes on each system will allow patrons to access a system without having to pay long distance or interzone telephone charges.

ASU and MCCCD linked their integrated library systems several years ago using TCP/IP over a 56KB WESTNET link. Phoenix Public Library was added to the network as part of the grant (see Figure 2).

The final phase of the project will provide full-text document delivery of selected article images from a UMI Image Delivery Server. This jukebox server contains 240 CD-ROMs with over 7.2 million scanned pages from over 400 journal titles from 1987 to the present. A Unix-based request server will be developed as part of this application using C++. This client-server based application or "request server" will adhere to NISO Z39.50

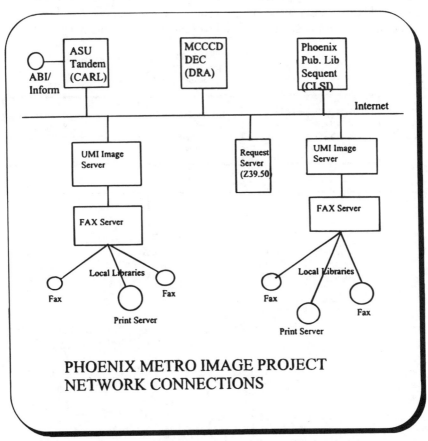

PHOENIX METRO IMAGE PROJECT NETWORK CONNECTIONS

Figure 2. Phoenix Metro Image Project network connections

standards and will be easily transportable to other Unix systems (see Figure 3).

The system will work in the following way. A user will approach a terminal (or dial-in with a PC) to any of the three library OPACs (CARL, CLSI, or DRA). Once the ABI/INFORM database is selected, the user will be automatically connected to the database loaded on the CARL system at ASU. A search is performed and if an article has a full-text image available, the citation will be flagged. The article may then be requested, at which time the user will again be connected to the Unix request server that will ask where the article should be faxed (to a library, office, or home); some financial questions will be asked, and then the request will go to the UMI Image Server that will deliver the article using traditional fax technology.

The Internet provides the backbone for intersystem OPAC connection and also connectivity between the CARL system at ASU and the Unix request server that will query, stack-up, and feed requests to the Image Server. Using this technique, additional request servers and image servers could be placed anywhere in the state or country and faxes could be sent to local or regional phone num-

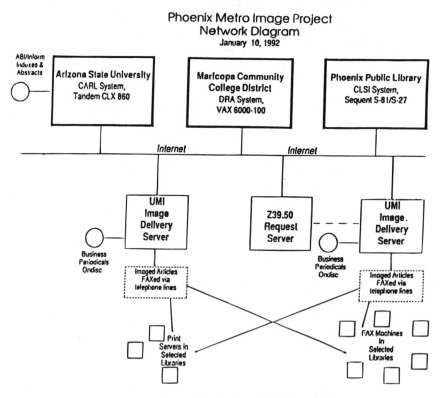

Figure 3. Phoenix Metro Image Project network diagram

bers. Because the bottleneck in this scenario is the CD-ROM jukebox image server, it will be easy to assess load and add additional servers when necessary.

Issues

Offering broad public and institutional access to the Internet comes with a set of issues. These include the following:

- Building and maintaining a campus computer and telecommunications infrastructure to support fast growing needs.
- Providing adequate security to make sure that registered users gain access and to minimize exposure to hackers on both ASU computers and other computer systems around the country.
- Developing institutional policies, procedures, and forms to make it clear what kind of access is available to whom and to minimize ASU and new user hassle. Because of the complexity to levels of access, interested users must still call and discuss their needs with an individual before appropriate forms are sent.
- In the libraries and the computer center, appropriate levels of service must be defined. For example, users may get into many different library systems through the CARL OPAC but in many of these systems, the user must proceed at his/her own risk because local staff cannot be up-to-date on every change in remote systems.
- Deciding what library systems to gateway from the CARL OPAC.

Conclusion

Personal and institutional access to the Internet may be gained through many different techniques: universities, private companies, consortia, and others. Public universities play a unique role in this regard—either as an aggressive advocate of network connectivity in their sphere of influence or at the other extreme they may take the role of isolationist, offering access to their primary clientele. People need access and it is now available from many different sources. Universities can choose to be a player or to watch from the sidelines as others provide the connectivity.

BUBL, the Bulletin Board for Libraries

Dennis Nicholson
Library Systems Officer
Strathclyde University
Glasgow, Scotland

I n June 1993 I was asked to write a chapter for this book on BUBL. For various reasons the publication was held up so that in August 1994 I was asked to write a supplement. In attempting this, however, I quickly realized that the only part of the chapter that had not been turned on its head in the intervening fourteen months was the historical part. The chapter as I wrote it in June 1993 is presented below and is followed by an attempt to describe the changes that have taken place between then and now. Hopefully, the contrast between the two parts makes an interesting commentary on the speed with which the virtual library is evolving. Remember though, that "now" is August 1994. If you are reading this at a much later date, don't stake your reputation on things being the same. This is the Internet, folks. Nothing will ever be "the same" again!

BUBL is the Bulletin Board for Libraries, an information service for librarians on JANET, the Joint Academic Network in the United Kingdom. It was originally set up as an experimental service under Project Jupiter—the aim of which was to train library staff in the use of JANET. BUBL is currently maintained, on behalf of JUGL (the JANET User Group for Libraries) by a team of volunteers based mainly at the two universities in Glasgow. The service runs on a DEC (Digital Equipment Corporation) VAX under VMS (Virtual Memory System) at the University of Glasgow, which provides machine facilities and software support free of charge.

Most of the information updates and additions are handled by a team based at Strathclyde University in the same city. Unfunded since the end of the Jupiter project, the service has recently attracted partial funding through

Figure 1. BUBL Welcome screen

a grant from the Information Systems Committee of the Universities Funding Council and through sponsorship (OCLC and Mecklermedia). However, it continues to rely mainly on volunteer effort.

BUBL hosts information of interest to network-using librarians. A major aim is to provide library networkers with information on services and resources available on JANET and other networks (e.g., IXI and the Internet). However, BUBL also covers items of general interest to librarians (the contents pages of library and information science journals, for example). It is, moreover, increasingly used by non-librarians—academics and students—for the guidance it provides on finding and using networked resources and services. It can be accessed over JANET (as GLA.BUBL or 00007110004011), over IXI (as 20433450710511), or from the Internet: telnet SUN.NSF.AC.UK or 128.86.8.7, login: janet. At the hostname:prompt type UK.AC.GLA.BUBL (see Figure 1).

Coverage and Facilities

Figure 2 shows the BUBL main menu screen in September 1992, with sixteen major subsections displayed. A brief description of some of these subsections will give some idea of BUBL's coverage:

B. Electronic reference works of various kinds, including manuals, guides, descriptions of networked services, bibliographies of networking, subject-based resource guides

C. Recent library and information science publications with abstracts (courtesy of BOOKDATA and others)

D. National and international e-text directories covering OPACs, information services, e-mail addresses, scholarly discussion lists, and resources in general

E. The most recent contents pages of over seventy library and information science journals

```
---*****MAIN MENU*****---

A--All about BUBL              J--Glossary
B--Reference Section           K--Practical exercises
C--New titles in LIS           L--British Library R &D News
D--Directories               **N--Latest changes to BUBL
E--Current Contents            O--CONCISE(Pan-European Inf.Serv.)
F--Mailing lists               S--Electronic Journals & Texts
G--NISS                        V--Library Systems & Software
H--Users' board                Z--CTILIS


***----------------*******Special Features*******--------------***
*  Section D1:   New (interim) edition of JANET OPACS          *
*                (compiled by Peter Stone)                     *
*  Section Z3E : US software held at CTILIS(Loughborough)      *
***************************************************************
* POST PROBLEMS? - Section A9 may have the answer...          *
***-------------------------------------------------------***
```

Options: HELP HINTS SEARCH MAIL POST QUIT M (Main Menu) or <RETURN> (Next Page)
Please select section name, page number or option :

Figure 2. Main menu

H. Users information, including information from library and information science organizations, news, items for sale, results of surveys

S. Electronic journals and texts, including sources of electronic texts, a directory of electronic journals and newsletters, some electronic journals in the library and information science field, and related items

V. Library systems and software items

Z. Special user education section run by the Loughborough University CTILIS team

Figure 2 also shows, along the bottom of the screen display, the various facilities offered by the USERBUL software, which provides BUBL's user interface. USERBUL allows information to be accessed through a series of menus and submenus. However, because the hierarchical structure is apparent rather than real, users need not "climb" or "descend" through the menus to reach the files or menus and submenus in which they are interested.

Providing they know what section or sub-section they require, they need simply type in its designator and press Return to display the electronic document that interests them. Once a document has been retrieved, the user may browse through it a screen at a time by pressing Return at the end of each screen, or may jump to a particular page by typing in the page number and pressing Return. A simple search facility is available for searching large documents such as directories, or manuals, or major resource guides. Other facilities offered by the software are the following:

HELP, HINTS, SEARCH - Simple help screen displays

MAIL - Send a message to the BUBL team

POST - Send documents to your own e-mail box

This, then, describes BUBL as it is today (September 1992). The remainder of the chapter looks at the beginnings of BUBL as a Project Jupiter experimental service and at its development into an operational service run by a group of volunteers and its subsequent rise in popularity. The chapter also covers ongoing plans to secure BUBL's long-term future, with particular reference to a BLRDD-funded investigation into how BUBL's role and, consequently, its coverage and facilities, should be developed over the next few years.

Beginnings

At the very beginning, JANET came into being in 1984 and has since become a vital part of U.K. academic and research activity. JANET provides users with access to over 2,000 U.K. computers at universities, research council institutes, and a selection of other educational institutions, and commercial and industrial sites. It also links them to other networks, such as the Internet, IXI, and PSS/IPSS. With over seventy U.K. library catalogues, numerous databases, and information services, and a selection of library supplier sites accessible over JANET, as well as access to international information services, databases, and library catalogues, librarians are a significant user group. They are represented within the JANET community by JUGL, the JANET User Group for Libraries.

JUGL came into being in 1986 with an original charge to comment on the quality of the network service. It quickly extended its sphere of interest, however, and now has much wider aims, summarized in this extract from its policy statement of 24 April 1991:

> The JANET User Group for Libraries (JUGL) encourages the use of the Joint Academic NETwork (JANET) by libraries and their users, acts as a forum for discussion of their use of the network, and makes proposals for its further development. It aims to assist in the development and training of the library profession in the effective use of the network, and promotes standards and service objectives for new forms of information dissemination.

Libraries eligible to connect to JANET are automatically members of JUGL and may vote in the annual election of JUGL committee members. Over the years, a succession of active, innovative, and hard-working committee members have helped make JUGL a significant force, both in terms of encouraging libraries and librarians to use and exploit JANET, and in terms of promoting library interests within the wider network community.

This is not an appropriate place to detail all of the activities and successes of JUGL. Some further detail may be found in "JANET: The Educational and Research Network of the United Kingdom," by Peter Stone,[1] who has played a major role in the group. It is sufficient to note here that JUGL's influence on the early history of BUBL was twofold. First, it helped encourage and foster the library networking community that BUBL would ultimately serve—by holding workshops and conferences, by publishing the quarterly JUGL newsletter, and by compiling and distributing a directory of e-mail addresses of all JANET libraries, among other things. Second, it was successful in obtaining funding for Project Jupiter, the project that gave rise to BUBL.

Project Jupiter was a two-year research project funded by the University Grants Committee in 1989 and 1990. JUGL called for tenders from university libraries and subsequently accepted the proposals put forward by Glasgow University Library. The project began in February 1989 and was managed by Andrew Wale, the deputy librarian. It had three aims:

1. To arrange a series of seminars throughout the United Kingdom on the use of networks, and JANET in particular
2. To produce a guide for libraries on JANET.
3. To investigate the feasibility of a bulletin board for libraries.

The last of these led to the setting up of a prototype BUlletin Board for Libraries, called BUBL.

BUBL was set up in early 1990 by the first Jupiter project officer, John MacColl, and was developed further under the second project officer, Margaret Isaacs. Because it was impossible to guarantee support for the service once Jupiter ended, and, in any case, it was not known for certain whether there was a role for such a service to play, it was decided that it should be approached as an experiment: "a test of the viability and desirability of an interactive online information service, specifically on library-related matters" as Margaret Isaacs put it in her report on the project.[2] The service was set up on Glasgow University's VAX, utilizing a software package called USERBUL, developed at Leicester University, also in use on two other U.K. bulletin boards, NISSBB and HUMBUL. An e-mail discussion list (called BUBL, subsequently LIS-BUBL) was also set up to provide a forum for discussion of the service, to obtain user feedback, and to carry bulletins on new additions and updates to the service.

By the time Project Jupiter came to an end in July 1991, it had become clear that BUBL was welcomed by the library networking community and regarded as useful. Over the previous sixteen months, a wide range of material had been made available on the bulletin board. Some of this was related specifically to library networking—for example, the Jupiter *Guide for Libraries on JANET*,[3] the Jupiter workshop exercises, directories of JANET OPACs and library e-mail numbers, information on JANET information services and e-mail lists, and so on. The remainder was of wider interest—abstracts of new library and information science monographs (provided by the library supplier BOOKDATA from its CD-ROM), contents pages from Library and information science journals, information on research projects funded by the BLRDD, and others.

From August 1990 onward (four months after BUBL was set up), usage levels were monitored. These showed a steady rise from about two logins per day in the early months, to an average over the final six months of about twelve a day, with logins in the last six months averaging between 200 and 300 per month. This showed a steady and sustained level of interest in the service, an impression also confirmed by user feedback, with schools of library and information science showing a particular interest.

It appeared that there were reasonable grounds for concluding that an online information service covering specifically library-related matters did have a role to play in the library networking community—that BUBL was not only viable, but was regarded as desirable.

The experimental service had been a success. It was, however, only an experimental service, its existence entirely dependent on the Jupiter funding. With the end of this funding imminent, and no new source of funding available, it was unclear how the service could be continued, given that it was initially only an experiment. At this stage, Isaacs, the Jupiter project officer, sent an e-mail message to the library networking community explaining the position and asking whether anyone was interested in helping. A reply was received from a team of volunteers at Strathclyde University Library, just a few miles away in the same city. After some discussion, it was agreed that an attempt would be made to maintain BUBL as a cooperative venture. A team from Strathclyde University Library and elsewhere (see Figure 3), led by Dennis Nicholson of Strathclyde University, would be responsible for content, editorial control, and information dissemination. Glasgow University would continue to provide machine facilities and software support through Ian Walker (technical support person for BUBL in the Computer Centre at Glasgow University) and Andrew Wale (deputy librarian, Glasgow University Library) would continue to provide administrative advice and support. As a result, BUBL was re-launched soon after the end of Jupiter, this time with the stated aim of turning it into an operational service with a long-term future.

New Beginnings

Experimental or not, BUBL was already a significant information service by the end of Jupiter. Of the sixteen main sections now shown on the BUBL main menu (see Figure 2), twelve already existed in July 1991 (although many of these have been greatly expanded in content since then). At the foot of the screen shown in Figure 2, the facilities provided under the present version of USERBUL are shown. Of these, all but POST were already available in the version running in July 1991. Because the new BUBL editorial team was volun-

```
+--------------------------+
|     Section Editors      |
+--------------------------+
```

Current Contents(E)	-- Kenneth McMahon, Strathclyde University
Directories(D)	-- Jean Shaw, Strathclyde University
Electronic Journals & Texts(S)	-- Gill Morris, Strathclyde University
	(with DN)
Hot News(H1F)	-- Janet Peattie, Strathclyde University
New Titles in LIS(C)	-- Catherine Nicholson, Glasgow Polytechnic
Other sections	-- Dennis Nicholson, Strathclyde University

Contributors to Section E(Current Contents:

Kenneth, McMahon, Philip Calvert, Liz Chapman, Lorcan Dempsey, Alison McNab, Ann O'Brien, Glenis Pickering, Mary Sillitto, David Stoker, Peter Walsh

Figure 3. BUBL team

teers, working in their own spare time, it was not at all clear what level of service they would be able to provide. The team's initial aim, therefore, was to discover to what extent it would be possible to maintain the level of service achieved under Jupiter. In any event, this proved less difficult than had been imagined. It was necessary to reduce the number of documents created manually to a bare minimum (although Kenneth McMahon, editor of the Current Contents section, maintained and subsequently increased substantially his output in this area). However, it quickly became clear that reductions in the level of service in this area could be compensated for by increasing the coverage of documents already in electronic form—documents of interest but relatively inaccessible to most users in ftp archives, listserver mailstores and the like. A reasonable service could be maintained—and even improved—by a team of enthusiastic part-time volunteers.

Having achieved this vital initial goal, the team then began considering the longer term aim of making BUBL not just an operational service, but an operational service with a stable and long-term future. Initially, it was assumed that there were two requirements for this: (1) a larger, more stable user base, to be brought about by various means, including improvements in coverage and facilities; and (2) a reliable source of funding (or, more likely, several such sources). It was recognized that the two were interrelated. An increased user base depended partly on improving coverage and facilities, and this, in turn, depended to some extent on attracting financial support. Equally, BUBL would be better able to attract financial support if it could be proved that even under a team of volunteers the service was worth having and keeping and had a strong and growing user base. It was also subsequently recognized that the two requirements jointly gave rise to a third. Although some progress could be made without it, a coherent development plan, based on extensive and detailed research, would ultimately be required to guide service development into appropriate areas and to provide support and vital detail for funding applications.

Building the User Base

Attempts to increase the number of regular users of the BUBL service took several forms.

Increased Coverage

Attempts to increase coverage had to be carefully controlled. Given that the BUBL team was working on a voluntary basis, it was essential that any extension of BUBL's coverage was sustainable. Nevertheless, much was achieved in regards to the extension of coverage. In summary:

Section B was greatly expanded, the number of documents increasing fourfold. Additions included items on gopher, WAIS, CWIS resource requirements, bibliographies, descriptions of Network News, subject guides to Internet resources, and many others.

Section E was greatly expanded so that it now covers the contents pages of a significant number of library and information science periodicals.

Section D, the directories section, was expanded to cover a number of Internet directories as well as the JANET directories previously covered.

Section H, the "user board," was expanded in a number of areas to cover many more library and information science organizations and user groups, surveys, jobs, items for sale, electronic texts in user education, and others.

Section O was added. This gives details of the CONCISE pan-European information service and how to access and use it.

Section S was added. This covers electronic texts and electronic journals and newsletters, including the full text of some library and information science electronic journals.

Section V was added, covering library-related systems and software—various items including Gord Nickerson's LibSoft archive, and sample operational requirements from various sources.

Section Z was added, covering the cooperative user education project run by Jack Meadows and Fytton Rowland, the CTILIS (Computers in Teaching Initiative Library and Information Science) team at Loughborough University.

Improved Facilities

An upgrade of the USERBUL software was obtained and installed. The major new feature of this was that it enabled BUBL users to POST documents back to their own mailboxes by e-mail. This proved very popular.

Additional Access Routes

The team arranged for BUBL to become one of the options on the NISS (National Information on Software and Services) gateway on JANET. This boosted usage by 500 accesses per month in the one month for which comparative figures are available. In addition, IXI access (the European International X.25 Infrastructure) was arranged and publicized as was access from the Internet through the NSFnet relay service when this became available.

Information Dissemination Improvements

Under Jupiter, information on updates and additions to BUBL were sent out to the members of the BUBL (later LIS-BUBL) e-mail discussion list. This had fewer than one hundred members by the end of Jupiter. LIS-BUBL was one of many LIS (Library and Information Science) lists running at the time under the NISP (Networked Information Services Project) mailbase software at the University of Newcastle. These LIS lists had a master list (LIS-All) that allowed messages to be sent to all members of all LIS lists. For a time, LIS-All was used in preference to LIS-BUBL in an attempt to reach a broader selection of potential users. This had two problems:

1. People who were on various LIS lists under slightly different addresses received two, sometimes three, copies of each BUBL update message, causing extreme irritation in some cases.
2. It was impossible to be a member of a LIS list and not be a member of LIS-All, and some members objected to being "force-fed" BUBL updates.

It was therefore necessary to cease this practice and switch back to LIS-BUBL. However, the success of the basic strategy was proven in the process of this failed experiment. After the switch back to LIS-BUBL, the number of members of LIS-BUBL almost doubled. Consequently, when in late 1991 a merger of various LIS lists was planned with a view to creating a LIS superlist that did not have the disadvantages of LIS-All, LIS-BUBL took part in the merger. As a result, BUBL updates are now sent out to over 700 members of the new general list, LIS-Link. Figure 4 shows part of a typical BUBL update message.

Promotion of the Service

Every opportunity to improve the image and to raise the profile of the service was taken. Successes were reported, sponsorship and other deals were highlighted, increased usage figures were broadcast. An attempt was

```
         LATEST UPDATE/ADDITIONS TO BUBL
         ================================

04 Sep, 1992: Section H1ZC added RARE WG-ISUS Newsletter
              8-92

04 Sep, 1992: Section B70 added - SURFnet Guide
              (Netherlands)

04 Sep, 1992: Section VC2 updated - LIBSOFT Archive
              Recent Additions
              Section S16 updated - IRLIST Digest
              Section S5 updated - Project Guttenberg
              Newsletter
              Section V01B added - O.R. for the Templeman
              Library
              Section VC4 added - Internet Explorers'
              Toolkit
              Section Z3E added -  Software Packages Held
              at CITILIS
              Section Z3E1 added - Penrose Library,
              University of Denver
```

Figure 4. BUBL update message

made to make the library and information science community in the United Kingdom feel positive about BUBL and happy to be associated with it.

Increased Usage Statistics

That some or all of these efforts were successful is clear from the usage statistics. As indicated above, log-ins in the last six months of Jupiter (to July 1991) showed an average of between 200 and 300 accesses a month. In August and September, they rose to 484 and 450, respectively. In October, the first month on the NISS gateway, they rose to 1,117, with 549 through the gateway, but direct log-ins also increased to 568. In November, the figure rose again—to 1,260—but fell back to 962 in December (we are still trying to discover who got a modem for Christmas and logged in for twenty minutes on Christmas Day!). Thus, by the last three months of 1991, accesses were averaging between 962 and 1,260, four times the level under the last six months of Jupiter. Further increases were logged in 1992. The statistics are summarized in Figure 5.

Attempts to Secure Funding

As had been hoped, this growth in the user base helped to convince potential sponsors and funding bodies that BUBL was worthy of financial support. Although much remains to be done in this respect, efforts to attract funding have been sufficiently successful, both to allow service improvements to be introduced and to encourage the team to re-double their efforts

BUBL accesses per month: 1991

Jun'91	Jul'91	Aug'91	Sep'91	Oct'91	Nov'91	Dec'91
198	288	484	450	1117	1260	962

BUBL accesses per month: 1992

Jan'92	Feb'92	Mar'92	Apr'92	May'92	Jun'92	Jul'92
1366	1679	1808	1295	1546	1971	1650

Figure 5. Usage statistics chart

to secure additional financial support. Support for the day-to-day running of the bulletin board has come from two sources. The Information Systems Committee of the Universities Funding Council has contributed £4,000 to help support the service in the current financial year, and this has been supplemented by the contribution of smaller amounts by OCLC Europe and Mecklermedia Ltd. (U.K.). The OCLC sponsorship is particularly encouraging in that it is spread over three years and should help support at least the present level of service well into 1995. Funding for the ongoing support of the service is to be used to employ library school students to work part-time on bulletin board activities. The first of these—Fiona Wilson, a postgraduate student from the information science department at the University of Strathclyde—is already in post.

The team has also been successful in attracting funding to support research aimed at planning a future course for BUBL. The British Library Research and Development Division (BLRDD) has recently made £11,000 available to fund a six-month study into the future development of the service. This study began in August 1992 and will run until January/February 1993. The project officer is Colin Raeburn, a graduate student from the information science department at Strathclyde University. An account of the aims of the project is given below.

Future Directions

The aims of the BLRDD study are to investigate how BUBL's role and, consequently, its coverage and facilities, should be developed in the next few years and to produce a coherent, coordinated, and costed short-to-medium term development plan as a guide to future efforts. The following general areas will be investigated.

The Role of BUBL in Academic Networking

This will entail an investigation into the relationship of BUBL to the following:

- JUGL, PLANET, LIS-Link, and library networkers in general
- Other network services such as NISS
- European and international perspectives
- Library organizations: LA, Aslib, IIS, and others
- Relationship to LAnet and to the public library sector

Development of Coverage, Facilities, User Base

This will attempt to answer a number of questions:

- What obvious gaps are there in present coverage?
- What are the limitations of the present structures and access facilities and what improvements are desirable?
- Are proposed improvements in structure and structure-related facilities practical?
- What are the requirements and expectations of the present user base?
- In what ways, if any, should coverage be widened to cover LIS interests not covered at present?
- Should BUBL aim to serve the library-related needs of academic networkers who are not information workers?
- What are the financial implications of any proposed developments in terms of computing overheads and BUBL support staff?

Improvements in Methods of Relevant Information Capture and Incorporation

Relevant questions here are the following:

- What weaknesses exist in the present methods of information capture and incorporation?
- What strengths exist in the present methods and could they be extended to improve methods in other areas?
- What possibilities exist for automating update processes?
- What additional problems are involved in increasing the coverage in the ways suggested by the study? Can these problems be resolved and, if so, how?

- Are proposed improvements practical?
- Are there cost implications to proposed improvements?

BUBL: Future Hardware and Software Requirements

- What medium-term development plans should be made for BUBL in hardware and software terms? Should there be a plan to move to portable Unix-based software for example?
- Does appropriate Unix-based BBS (Bulletin Board Services) software exist, and what does it cost?

Financial Implications, Sponsorship, Income Generation

- How do other bulletin boards finance their operations?
- Who are the potential sponsors of BUBL?
- What levels of sponsorship would they support?
- What advantages do potential sponsors see in sponsoring BUBL?
- What methods of income generation exist?
- Is financial support from library organizations a possibility?
- What non-library organizations might sponsor BUBL?

The intention is to produce a report covering consideration of, and incorporating conclusions on, all of the topics outlined above, and culminating in a set of costed, prioritized sub-objectives which would constitute BUBL's development plan for the next few years. This would give guidance on BUBL's future direction and role, and would be used:

- to improve BUBL content, organization, and facilities
- to target and influence potential sponsors
- to generate income by other means
- to support future research grant applications, if appropriate

At the time of this writing, this study is still in its early stages, and its outcome—and, hence, the precise shape of BUBL's future development—is largely unknown. A number of interesting possibilities are under discussion, however, and if sufficient funds can be attracted to support them, the next few years may see the introduction of some or all of the following developments:

1. The service will move to a new hardware platform to run under Unix. A new user interface will be installed, with gopher being a strong possibility. Facilities will be improved. Gopher is likely to be used to provide a relatively user-friendly gateway to a range of networked

services, including OPACs, information services, and ftp archives. Full-text searching of the entire databases is a possibility, as is consideration of a subject-based or classified approach to the service.

2. BUBL will continue to be an information and support service for U.K. librarians and will seek to greatly expand its coverage and activities in this area.

- More library-related organizations and groups will be encouraged to cooperate and provide data.
- A wider range of library and information science journals will be covered.
- More electronic journals will be held.
- Public librarians will be encouraged to put up data on the board.
- Library-related software packages will be held and distributed.
- There will be an increase in the cooperative document sharing activities already begun in areas such as user education and the writing of operational requirements.

3. BUBL may seek to extend its role so that it serves not just librarians but the academic user community they serve. Some academics already use the service for the information it provides on other network resources and services and how to access them. It is possible that BUBL will, in the future, seek to deliberately target this group with an extension of the current BUBL service. This would again entail the use of gopher or something similar to provide user-friendly gateway facilities to a range of network services.

4. With the implementation of SuperJANET imminent, and the increased bandwidth that that implies, BUBL may seek to develop so that it may take advantage of the new opportunities offered, looking to provide access not just to text, but to documents incorporating sound and graphics, videos, and multimedia programs.

Whether any of this will actually come about will, of course, depend on the willingness of funding bodies and sponsors to support the continued existence and continued development of the service, and this is very much an unknown at present. What is certain, however, is that BUBL will continue in some form for the forseeable future and will continue to support, encourage, and inform the small but growing band of U.K. library and information workers who are intent on learning the skills necessary to enable them both to exploit networks and their resources to the fullest extent, and to ensure that they have a role to play in the future provision and development of networked information services.

Supplement

The BUBL Information Service In August 1994

The following text consists of excerpts from various BUBL documents prepared during 1994 and shows the extent to which things have changed for BUBL in only a few short months. Most of it is taken from the recently produced BUBL leaflet. Note, in particular, that the address of the service has changed, partly because we have moved geographically, partly because we now provide (direct) telnet, gopher and World Wide Web access, as well as JANET access. Other points of interest are the new BUBL subject tree and the significant increase in access statistics. In June 1993, I was pleased to be able to report that access statistics had increased from around 200 a month to nearly 3,000 a month in two years. A year later I am able to report that monthly accesses are now ranging between 16,000 and 20,000 a month. This is at least partly due to the fact that we are now serving a wider audience— that is, we are an Internet information service run for the academic community by librarians as well as being a service for library and information science professionals.

Description of the BUBL Information Service

The BUBL Information Service serves U.K. library and information science professionals and the wider academic and research community that they support. The MAIN MENU gives a broad idea of coverage:

- BUBL Beginners, Updates, Contacts, News, Sponsors
- Library and Information Science on and via BUBL
- Internet Resources by Subject; Reference Tools, Electronic Texts and Journals
- BUBL's Latest Additions and Amendments (files only)
- The BUBL Subject Tree and CATRIONA Projects
- Keyword Searching: BUBL Files, Internet: Archie, Veronica, WAIS
- NISS, Mailbase, SALSER, HENSA, CONCISE, etc.
- Services by Type: OPACs, Gopher Jewels, Gophers, WWW, WAIS
- Networks and Networking: Tools, User guides, Training, etc.

Library and Information Science on BUBL

BUBL began life as the Bulletin Board for Libraries and its major aim is still to inform, support, educate, and represent the interests of the U.K. LIS community. Option 2 on the BUBL top-level menu leads to the Library and Information Science sub-menu, which includes the following:

- Information Networking
- New Publications in Library and Information Science
- Directories of Internet and LIS-oriented resources
- Current Contents of Computing and LIS Journals
- Electronic Mail Discussion Lists
- LIS: Services, Education, Surveys, News, Organizations
- LIS Glossaries, Acronyms and Definitions
- LIS Education, Including Network Use Exercises
- Electronic Journals and Texts
- Traditional Divisions of Librarianship
- Library Systems & Software Resources
- CTILIS: Computers in Teaching Initiative

BUBL is the U.K. LIS profession's way of coordinating its activities on the network. If you are not actively involved you should be! Much of the BUBL service is provided through voluntary contributions. Contributing to BUBL not only gives you a warm glow, it can also be of direct value in your work. Both of the following tasks can be easily fitted into a busy schedule:

As a SECTION EDITOR, in addition to providing a service to colleagues, you can develop a personal networked database in your area of expertise or provide a networked service for your group or organization.

As a SUBJECT SPECIALIST you can create a classified archive of sources and resources in a particular subject area for your own use and for the use of your classes and colleagues.

BUBL seeks to help LIS professionals exploit the enormous potential of academic networks in the areas of worksharing, cooperation, group coordination, and service provision. More details on how you can use BUBL to help yourself and others are in BUBL Sections AC06 & AC07.

BUBL for the Academic Community

Library and Information Science professionals utilize BUBL to provide the wider academic community with organized, structured, and user-friendly access to network services and resources. Choose option 3 on the BUBL main menu to access this aspect of the service. Areas covered include:

- BUBL Beginners: Contacts, Help, Hints, News, Latest Additions, Star Items
- BUBL Subject Tree
- Electronic Journals and Texts
- Employment Resources and Opportunities

- Grants available and Competitions You Can Win
- Major Networked Services
- Networking Groups on the Internet
- Networks and Networking
- Non-Networked Groups on BUBL
- Reference Sources: Acronyms, Directories, E-lists, Glossaries
- Software for Work and Education

Further resources are available via the BUBL World Wide Web server. BUBL is managed on behalf of JUGL by Strathclyde University Library, with administrative assistance from Glasgow University Library. The service is run from Strathclyde University in Glasgow, Scotland, but based in Bath, England.

Access Statistics

LIS professionals and academics from all subject disciplines use BUBL. Usage is growing at an impressive rate:

Oct '93	Nov '93	Dec '93	Jan '94	Feb '94	Mar '94
7944	11,034	9494	13,077	16,141	20,076

BUBL has users in the U.K., Eire, most other European countries, the U.S., Canada, Australia, New Zealand, Japan, Hong Kong, Taiwan, Israel, and many others.

Access to BUBL

```
JANET X.29:  UK.AC.BATH.BUBL or 00006012101300
Telnet:      BUBL.BATH.AC.UK or 138.38.32.45    login: bubl
Gopher:      BUBL.BATH.AC.UK or 138.38.32.45    Port: 7070
WWW:         http://www.bubl.bath.ac.uk/BUBL/home.html
```

LIS-link

BUBL Updates are sent out regularly on LIS-link electronic mail discussion lists. To join LIS-link, send an e-mail message to:

```
mailbase@uk.ac.mailbase
```

leave the subject field blank, but put into the text field:

```
join LIS-link <first name> <surname>
example: join LIS-link John Brown
```

Instructions for Using BUBL

(Note: There is no longer a single set of instructions for using BUBL. Those shown here apply to JANET and telnet users of the BUBL gopher service. JANET and telnet users of the BUBL WWW service require slightly different instructions and, of course, those utilizing client-server access to the gopher and web servers have their own instructions.)

Moving around menus:

```
Up arrow  . . . . . . . . .: Move to previous line.
Down arrow  . . . . . . . .: Move to next line.
Right arrow, Return  . . .: Select menu choice.
Left arrow, u  . . . . . .: Go up a level.
>, +, Pgdn, space-bar  . .: View next menu.
<, -, Pgup, b  . . . . . .: View previous menu.
0-9  . . . . . . . . . . .: Select a numbered item.
m  . . . . . . . . . . . .: Return to the main menu.
q  . . . . . . . . . . . .: Exit from BUBL.
```

Moving around documents:

```
Right arrow, Return  . . .: Display.
f, Space bar  . . . . . . .: Move down a page.
b  . . . . . . . . . . . .: Move up a page.
q  . . . . . . . . . . . .: Quit document.
/(keyword)  . . . . . . . .: Search document.
```

E-mailing documents to yourself:
Display document to end or press q to quit, then press m. Enter your e-mail address in the form:

```
bob@vax.university.ac.uk
```

Client-server BUBL:
The instructions above apply only to JANET pad and Telnet access to BUBL. If you are using a gopher or World Wide Web client follow the instructions provided with that client. Client-server access brings many benefits, including the ability to display images, play sounds, and save documents to disk. There is more information on clients in section BE of BUBL.

Contact Information

(Note: Since this was written, Fiona Wilson has left BUBL. Joanne Wood, her replacement, is not yet in post, but will have the same e-mail address.)

Dennis Nicholson, Coordinating Editor: (d.m.nicholson@strath.ac.uk)
Fiona Wilson, Information Officer: (cijs19@vaxb.strath.ac.uk)
Jean Shaw: (cijs05@vaxb.strath.ac.uk)
Kenneth McMahon: (cijs08@vaxb.strath.ac.uk)
Andrew Wale: (a.wale@cms.glasgow.ac.uk)
Tel—041-552-3701 ext 4632
Fax—041-552-3304 (mark FAO: BUBL)

Contributions to BUBL are gratefully received and should be sent to cijs27@vaxb.strathclyde.ac.uk preferably in ASCII format. If you want to submit items in another format please contact BUBL first.

Service Improvements in 1994

Major ways in which we have improved the service include:

- the development of a full subject tree, the only fully developed tree offered by a U.K. National service, the only one to offer gopher and WWW client-server access as well as X.29 and telnet, and to combine gopher and WWW services and resources in a single tree
- increased use of facilities by the LIS community, with sixteen section editors maintaining their own BUBL sections over e-mail and seventeen subject specialists (shared with NISS), helping to build the subject tree
- telnet access now available
- experimental lynx access allowing JANET and telnet users access to WWW
- improvement in the number of LIS journals covered in the current contents section of BUBL
- over 5,000 gopher links to Internet services and resources by mid-year
- hundreds of links added to the WWW server in 1994
- longer LIS-link current awareness bulletins
- major menu re-organization
- significant increase in e-mail lists monitored (eighty-three now covered world-wide)
- creation of LIS-SYS to encourage systems librarians to work-share by jointly maintaining a BUBL systems librarians' section

The Aims of the BUBL Information Service

BUBL's primary aim is to encourage, develop, coordinate and support the emerging LIS networking community in the U.K. and to promote its interests. Arising out of this primary aim are BUBL's secondary aims:

- to establish a clear and recognized role for LIS professionals in the provision and development of network-based library and information services
- to encourage the involvement of LIS professionals in new and existing network projects
- to encourage LIS professionals to exploit the network and network service for professional purposes such as cooperation, work-sharing, communication, and publishing
- to encourage LIS professionals to exploit the network for service provision purposes and encourage the creation, development, and improvement of such services
- to provide the wider academic community with information on an organized access to network resources and services
- to provide access to training materials and information on other network training initiatives
- research, development, service provision, and publishing related to BUBL's various aims
- to provide the LIS networking community with current awareness and archive information storage and retrieval services appropriate to BUBL's various aims
- to secure the long-term future of the service

References

1. Stone, Peter. "JANET: The Educational and Research Network of the United Kingdom." In *Wide-area Network Applications in Libraries*, ed. by Gregory Zuck and Bruce Flanders. Westport, CT: Meckler, 1992.
2. Isaacs, Margaret. "Project Jupiter: Report and Assessment." *Journal of Librarianship and Information Science* 24, no. 1 (1992): 15–22.
3. Isaacs, Margaret and John MacColl. *Guide for Libraries on JANET.* Glasgow: Project Jupiter, 1991.

Developing Access to Electronic Texts in the Humanities

Susan Hockey
Director, Center for Electronic Texts in the Humanities
Rutgers and Princeton Universities
New Brunswick and Princeton, New Jersey

The Challenges of Electronic Texts

E lectronic texts are becoming major scholarly resources in the humanities, but as yet we have almost no recognized procedures or standards for providing access to the texts or for maintaining them for the long term. The natural tendency is first to attempt to treat electronic texts in the same way that we treat books. But they are a new medium that is dynamic in nature, and one that we do not yet fully understand. This chapter will survey the issues that need to be considered to establish a better methodology for handling these new resources in the humanities.

Primary source material in the humanities may be literary works, historical documents, manuscripts, papyri, inscriptions, coins, transcriptions of spoken texts, or dictionaries, and it can be in any natural language. Most scholarly activity in the humanities is concerned with interpreting primary source material and publishing those interpretations in secondary sources such as monographs and journals, with reference to earlier interpretations of the same source. Here we are concerned with electronic versions of the source material, and the term electronic text is used here to mean a transcription of source material into computer-readable form, letter by letter and character by character, including whatever additional information is needed to make the text useful. This format allows the words within the text to be searched and otherwise manipulated by computer programs, in contrast to electronic image format in which a picture of the source material can be reproduced, enhanced, or rotated, but not otherwise manipulated by a program. The text format thus provides the flexibility for many more applications in humanities scholarship. In the longer term we can expect source material to be available in both image and text format, but much of the discussion in this paper is concerned with the particular challenges of electronic texts.

For the last thirty years or so humanities scholars have used electronic texts for many scholarly applications. These include concordances and word frequency indexes for print publication, analyses of style and authorship based on vocabulary usage, the production of historical dictionaries, other applications involving lexis and some simple forms of syntax and morphology, and producing scholarly editions. Collections of textual material such as the *Anglo-Saxon Corpus*, the *Global Jewish Database*, or the *Thesaurus Linguae Graecae*, which can be searched very rapidly, also provide valuable reference material for historians, archaeologists, and anthropologists. More recently hypertext systems, which permit links between associated, yet randomly distributed, items of information have been used as teaching tools. For example, hypertext systems are used to show images of the art, architecture, and geography of Ancient Greece as in the Perseus project, or even to model the narrative structures of literature.

An electronic text may be either (1) in a form that can be displayed, printed, or otherwise manipulated by whatever software an individual chooses to use or write (often called a plain text or ASCII file), or (2) in a form that is indexed or organized for specific software and therefore only usable with that software (usually as CD-ROMs). ASCII files can easily be copied, transmitted around the network, updated, and amended. They provide much more flexibility, provided that adequate software is available. It is estimated that over ninety-five percent of existing electronic texts in the humanities are in this format and have been created in an ad hoc fashion by individuals or research institutes for specific research projects. Examples include large historical dictionaries such as the *Trésor de la Langue Française* or *Hebrew Dictionary*, or individual research projects such as that performed by John Burrows on the novels of Jane Austen. A considerable body of expertise in handling these texts has been built up within the humanities, where the major forum for presenting new methodologies has become the joint annual conference of the Association for Literary and Linguistic Computing and the Association for Computers and the Humanities. It is only very recently that libraries have begun to think about acquiring texts in this form and to consider how they might handle them and make them available. The natural tendency is to attempt to adapt or extend the tools used for handling static print material to electronic resources, but these tools are, for the most part, not so well suited to deal with dynamic electronic material.

The remaining five percent or so of texts represent mostly commercially available products such as the CD-ROM from CETEDOC (Centre de Traitement Électronique des Documents at Louvain-la-Neuve, Belgium), which contains works of the early Christian fathers, or the *New Oxford English Dictionary*, or texts for use with the WordCruncher text searching program, which is marketed by Johnston and Company of Utah. Some of these were developed in the academic world, such as the CETEDOC CD-ROM. Others, such as the CD-ROMs of the *Patrologia Latina* from Chadwyck-Healey, are entirely commercial ventures. It is these texts that are most often found in libraries, particularly those on CD-ROM, which are most appropriate for the current, mainly print-based, library environments.

The body of experience that has been built up shows that a raw text without any additional information encoded within it is of little use for scholarly purposes. When features such as author, title, chapter, page, and other characteristics such as quotations, proper names, foreign words, or even parts of speech, are marked or specially identified in some way, electronic texts become much more useful. This is because a word that is retrieved can be located exactly in the page or chapter, etcetera, within which it occurs, or a search can be performed, for example, on all quotations within a text or on all names. There are at least thirty different methods for encoding such additional information in use for plain text files, many of which are not well documented. However, a major international initiative has tackled this problem and produced guidelines for a common format.

A number of organizations provide electronic texts or information about texts, of which three are worthy of mention here. The Center for Text and Technology at the Georgetown University Academic Computing Center has compiled a catalog of projects in electronic text. The catalog lists some 300 projects and institutions that hold electronic texts. The information provided includes contact persons, primary discipline focus, language, intended use, size of texts, and mode of access. It does not include any information about the individual texts that each project holds. The Oxford Text Archive (OTA) was established at Oxford University Computing Services in 1976 to "offer scholars long term maintenance of electronic versions of literary and linguistic texts and to manage the distribution of electronic texts and information about them to the scholarly community." It is committed to maintaining any text that is deposited in it, but does not itself actively pursue adding material. The OTA has nearly a thousand texts in some twenty-five languages, predominantly English, but makes no guarantee about the condition of the texts, which are in many different formats without any standards for minimum encoding or error verification. Some texts are freely available and accessible by ftp, or for a nominal cost, on disk or tape. Others are available only by written authorization of the depositor. All are plain ASCII files and require the user to provide appropriate software. The *Thesaurus Linguae Graecae* (*TLG*) at Irvine, California, is the one major systematic attempt to compile a comprehensive collection of literature in one language. It incorporates all works in Ancient Greek from the time of Homer to 600 A.D., which form some sixty million words, and is now nearing completion. The *TLG* is licensed to individuals and institutions and is distributed on CD-ROM. The encoding format, devised when the project began in 1972, is somewhat idiosyncratic. The texts are not indexed, but are plain ASCII files, which require special purpose software for searching.

Documentation of electronic texts is also somewhat scarce. The text archives held in research institutes usually have a style manual or code book describing their particular encoding scheme and perhaps also some documentation of the source material, but many individual texts have little or no documentation either of the specific encoding scheme or of the source edition used. There has been very little use either of bibliographic records to document electronic texts or of documentation maintained as part of the electronic text file. Both of these are deemed essential for multi-purpose scholarly access to the texts.

An additional problem for the dissemination of electronic texts is that the copyright situation on many existing texts is unclear. Although there are now reasonably well-established guidelines for copyright permissions for electronic texts, many electronic texts have been compiled without permission and their compilers are thus reluctant to advertise their existence. The copyright problem has been compounded by the ease of movement of texts from one country to another over the network for which there are no internationally recognized guidelines. International efforts are needed to rectify this situation for existing and future scholarly texts in the humanities.

It was in recognition of all of these issues that the Center for Electronic Texts (CETH) was established by Rutgers and Princeton in 1991. Until then, in North America, there had been no concerted effort to bring the use of electronic texts into the center of the scholarly arena by building on existing resources and "know-how". Electronic texts need to be accessible to any scholar or institution through the library environment in a standard or recognized form, which will supplement and enhance the traditional modes of humanities scholarship. The center's mission is to take a leading role in formulating effective methodologies for developing, maintaining, and using electronic texts created by individual scholars or projects. It will achieve this objective by setting up a consortium of member institutions that will work together to establish a framework for advancing scholarship in the humanities by the use of high-quality electronic texts.

Cataloging Electronic Texts

Because most electronic texts have been compiled for specific projects, it is not surprising that information about these texts is scarce. Those who have been responsible for compiling electronic texts generally have not had any experience with using bibliographic records for cataloging the texts. Because no other ground rules exist, they have developed their own ad hoc procedures for documenting the texts. Some individuals have not documented the texts at all, because the information they need for using the texts is already built into their own special purpose software.

The only attempt to create a systematic catalog using standard bibliographic procedures is the Rutgers Inventory of Machine-Readable Texts in the Humanities, which has now been taken over by CETH. The inventory was established by Rutgers in 1983 in response to a growing number of enquiries about the availability of electronic texts. It is a catalog of existing electronic texts in the humanities and is held on the Research Libraries Information Network (RLIN). By 1990 the Inventory had grown to some 800 records. At this stage funding was provided by the Mellon Foundation for a one-year post to catalog the Oxford Text Archive. A cataloger and archivist spent one year in Oxford and was able to collect and compile data sufficient to create catalog records for about 800 OTA texts. The cataloger used material provided by the depositors of the texts to determine the edition, etcetera, where possible, and then verified sixty lines each from the beginning, middle, and end of the text against the printed source in the Bodleian Library in an attempt to establish more information about the text.

In 1991 the National Endowment for the Humanities provided support for the cataloging of electronic texts at CETH, and a full-time cataloger started work in January 1992. The cataloger began by concentrating on those humanities texts that are available commercially, because it seemed sensible to give priority to those texts that are most readily available. CETH purchased the most widely-used ones, which were used for experimental cataloging and for helping the cataloger develop procedures for the cataloging.

There are a number of very obvious differences between cataloging print material and computer files. The content of a computer file cannot be seen without examining that file on a computer, and appropriate software is necessary for files that are not plain text. CETH has found that most of the expertise in cataloging computer files is derived from experience with either software or social science numeric data files. There seems to have been very little emphasis specifically on electronic text files. CETH is using the rules in chapter nine of the *Anglo-American Cataloging Rules*, second edition, 1988 Revision (AACR2R). These rules cover all kinds of computer files (programs, numeric data files, etc.), but are not especially suitable for electronic texts. For example, they specify a title screen, which most electronic texts do not have, because these texts are mostly plain text files without software to display any titling information. The physical characteristics of a file are also less important now because of the ease of copying from one medium to another, and we do not record this information except in the case of CD-ROM. However, we do consider it important to record information about the encoding scheme and whether the text needs specific software, because this information is necessary for any user of the text. It also seems sensible to provide a cross-reference to a catalog entry for the printed source from which an electronic text is derived. Furthermore, unlike most other catalog records on RLIN, very few of the items are owned by the cataloging institution (the center), which has to acquire information about them from their holders. It was, therefore, even more important to determine exactly what information was needed for the cataloging and to describe this in a way that is easily understood before attempting to elicit information from the holders or compilers of texts.

In contrast to the static form of a book, an electronic text is a dynamic object that can be amended and updated many times. As the inventory develops, there will be a need to establish procedures for determining what constitutes a new version and to amend existing records as new versions of those texts become available. As a first step in this direction, the CETH cataloger has analyzed the 800 non-OTA records. Of these, a substantial number were records from three research institutes. The remainder described texts that are listed as being in the hands of eighty-nine different private individuals, and we are now determining whether these individuals still have the texts and whether the texts have been updated.

At present the main source of information for updating the inventory is a survey that was developed under the guidance of Antonio Zampolli, the director of the Institute of Computational Linguistics, Pisa, and president of the Association for Literary and Linguistic Computing, and Donald Walker, director of Language and Knowledge Resources Research, Bellcore, and secretary-treasurer of the Association for Computational Linguistics. Professor Zampolli and Dr. Walker are widely acknowledged as being the two major international figures in text analysis computing. The survey has had input from a large number of people in the field and has undergone a number of revisions to ensure that it will provide the information needed. It is believed to represent the most exhaustive survey ever conducted of texts and associated resources in electronic form. It is intended to be comprehensive in its coverage on written language, spoken language, and dictionary and other lexical information. It also elicits a considerable amount of information that will be useful for long-term planning and development of text analysis computing on an international basis.

The survey began in 1990 with funding from the Commission of the European Çommunities. An initial questionnaire was distributed to some 5,000 people who were on the mailing lists of the Association for Literary and Linguistic Computing, the Association for Computers and the Humanities, the Association for Computational Linguistics, and twelve other sponsoring organizations. Recipients were asked to note which of the following types of data they held: (1) speech (tape recordings), (2) single (individual) texts, (3) collections of texts, (4) corpora (collections of texts that have been put together on a principled basis as samples that represent a specific population, e.g. the Brown Corpus), (5) machine-readable dictionaries, and (6) computational lexica. The intention was to send a different follow-up questionnaire depending on the type of data held. CETH has taken over responsibility for doing the follow-up for (2), (3), and (4). The follow-up has already been done by other groups for (5) and (6), and that for (1) is in progress elsewhere.

The second follow-up questionnaire formed three parts. Part A requested information about the hardware and software environment used. Part B was concerned with single texts and Part C merged (3) and (4) above. In re-designing the questionnaire CETH took great care to ensure that the responses were provided in such a way that bibliographic records could easily be created, although we recognized that many of the respondents would not be familiar with the use of bibliographic records for cataloging electronic texts. The questionnaire was accompanied by a covering letter from Zampolli and Walker stressing the need to complete it. The questionnaire was mailed to some 270 respondents who were on the initial mailing list during August 1992. The material they provided could then be used to refine the questionnaire further to seek information from other institutions and individuals.

The *Humanities Computing Yearbook* is the major source of information about humanities computing, and that together with the Georgetown catalog of projects can be used to select the next batch of questionnaire recipients. CETH also has information about the texts in the OTA that are still not cataloged. The indications are that there are already tens of thousands of electronic texts in the humanities. The combined holdings alone of ARTFL (American Research on the Treasury of the French Language), the *Thesaurus Linguae Graecae*, and the Institute of Computational Linguistics at Pisa number over 10,000. As more individuals realize the benefits of using electronic texts, it seems likely that the rate of compilation will increase. It therefore becomes all the more necessary to have a commonly acceptable method to document, catalog, and maintain these materials.

Once a standard method of documenting an electronic text within the text file is in use, we expect to speed up the cataloging process by extracting information automatically or semi-automatically from that documentation. Other organizations may also be able to contribute to cooperative cataloging, using the guidelines that CETH has established. We are making contact with traditional publishers, who are moving into the electronic texts market, to determine their procedures for obtaining cataloging information for electronic texts.

The cataloging will continue on RLIN, which is a major online source of bibliographic information, but it is recognized that this cannot be accessed everywhere. A master database of the Inventory will be maintained by CETH, from which it will be possible to generate the information in other forms and in particular to make it available over the Internet under terms still to be explored. A print publication is also planned.

The Text Encoding Initiative

CETH is also firmly committed to the use of a standard encoding format for electronic texts and is adopting the Text Encoding Initiative (TEI) guidelines in full. The TEI grew out of a need that was first recognized in the humanities and has since been extended to other types of texts and linguistic resources. It is a major international project sponsored by the Association for Computers and the Humanities, the Association for Computational Linguistics, and the Association for Literary and Linguistic Computing and has defined a common encoding format for interchange and for encoding new texts. It began with a planning meeting at Vassar College in November 1987 in which some thirty international representatives from universities and research institutes surveyed the current situation of many different encoding schemes, most of which are poorly documented and ill-suited for applications other than those for which they were originally devised. The meeting discussed the desirability and feasibility of a common set of guidelines for encoding electronic texts, and there was a firm consensus that such a common framework was necessary. The group agreed on several basic principles to govern the scope and organization of such new guidelines and charged two representatives from each of the three sponsoring organizations to form a steering committee to direct the project.

The TEI received funding from the National Endowment for the Humanities in 1988 and subsequently also from the Commission of the European Communities and the Andrew W. Mellon Foundation. It soon adopted the Standard Generalized Markup Language (SGML) as the basis of its encoding scheme. SGML became an international standard in 1986. It is not itself an encoding scheme, but provides a framework for an encoding scheme which is flexible, extensible and satisfactory for many scholarly needs. The principle of SGML is descriptive rather than prescriptive. It provides a mechanism that has a sound theoretical and intellectual basis for describing the characteristics of a text in such a way that many different functions can be performed on the text—these may include printing, searching, browsing, or hypertext links. By contrast, a prescriptive scheme specifies a function to be performed on the text, e.g., to print it in a given point size with specific fonts. For example, if a play is being encoded, each act, scene, and speech would need to be encoded and for each speech, the name of the speaker would be given as well. This enables a retrieval program to search separate elements of the text, for example, all the speeches by one person, and also to identify those words that have been retrieved by act, scene, etcetera. If the play is being printed, the speakers' names could be converted into italic or each act could begin on a new page.

The descriptive material for "singled out" text is embedded in the text in the form of tags that are enclosed by angle brackets. The set of tags that is permissible in a text and their relationship to each other are defined in a document type definition (DTD), which a program can use to parse or validate the tags in a text. The tags may also have additional information in the form of attribute values, for example, to denote the language if the tag is for a foreign word. The TEI makes extensive use of attribute values, for example, to specify the language of a section of text which is not in the main language of the text, but, more importantly, to provide cross-referencing to information that is elsewhere in the text or external to it.

From the outset the philosophy of the TEI has not been to define sets of tags that characterize particular types of text, but to make their use optional, the basic philosophy being "if you want to tag this feature, do it this way." A text may contain many tags or it may have very few, depending on the requirements and time and cost constraints of the compiler of the text. A later user of the text may of course add further tags. Following a distinction that was first discussed at the planning meeting, the TEI established four working committees. The Committee on Text Documentation is likely to be of most interest to this audience. It has produced recommendations for a header for each electronic text file. The header contains information that is necessary to catalog and document the file. The first component within the header is bibliographic information about the source (at present, normally a text that already exists in print) that conforms to the ISBD standard. This is followed by information about the encoding used within the text, indicating what features were encoded and why. The profile description provides further details about the project for which the text was encoded, and the last section of the header is the revision history, which documents all the changes made to the file.

The Committee on Text Representation dealt with problems of specifying the logical structure of the text, character sets, and other features that are represented physically in the source material. It also laid ground rules for encoding features that are common to most or all texts, e.g. quotations, lists, names, abbreviations, and bibliographic citations. The Committee on Text Analysis and Interpretation developed a number of mechanisms for encoding linguistic and other analytic structures. The fourth Committee on Metalanguage and Syntax Issues produced recommendations on how SGML might best be used by the TEI and suggested modifications in SGML that might be needed to accommodate the TEI.

The TEI produced the first draft of its guidelines as an interim report concentrating on the core requirements in July 1990. Since then the work of the documentation and syntax committees has continued. In the second development cycle beginning in July 1990 specific areas were addressed in detail by a number of small work groups. The topics they worked on included character sets, hypermedia, formulae and tables, literary prose, performance texts, drama, manuscripts, corpora, spoken texts, dictionaries, terminological data, historical studies, and general linguistics.

A second version of the TEI Guidelines was published in May 1994. This version is much more comprehensive in its approach and will provide a sound basis for further work that has already been identified in the areas of linguistic resources, dictionaries, spoken texts, and literature.

Besides the obvious reasons for standardization, encoding in SGML requires a thorough analysis of the intellectual issues involved in creating an electronic text. It provides a much better mechanism than any other encoding scheme for handling the complexities of scholarly texts in the humanities; for example, the critical apparatus, marginal notes, and changes of language and script, for which adequate encoding schemes have never previously been available. Notes can be linked to the main text as it is being searched, and separate indexes can easily be made for the different languages in a multilingual text. The TEI has developed mechanisms for encoding the results of linguistic analysis and other interpretive material (literary and historical), which permit more than one analysis to be given for a text. At some stage in the future we can expect new publications to be only electronic in form and to include these analyses and interpretations as layers above the basic text in such a way that they can be used or discarded as the reader or user of the text wishes.

Collecting and Disseminating Texts

The Text Collection is the second major activity within the center. Based on the collective experience that has been acquired by users of electronic texts in humanities computing over the last thirty or so years, we feel that the time has come to provide some good quality, reliable texts that have as much authority and integrity as printed and published works. This seems to be best done by concentrating on focused collections of material that are properly tagged and documented, that represent good scholarly editions, and that can be used for many different applications.

Concentrating on focused collections will help to fulfil our mission of making use of electronic texts central to humanities scholarship where users should expect the same quality of material as they find in a printed book or source, with adequate tools for accessing it. Before now many electronic texts have been in the public domain and of variable quality. But recently there have been moves towards better policy, acceptability, and control for electronic texts. A panel representing a publishing house, a scholar, a librarian, and the CETH director voiced considerable support for this approach at the joint conference of the Association for Literary and Linguistic Computing and the Association for Computers and the Humanities in Oxford held in April 1992. Making the material available through the library environment also implies permanence and standardization, which have been lacking in other attempts to collect and distribute electronic text. By maintaining the data centrally in one standard format, we will be able to ensure that it is preserved for the future in a usable form.

We expect to begin the Text Collection with the Women Writers Project. This project began at Brown University in 1989 and is creating a textbase of all women's writing in English for the period 1350–1830. It is an ideal test database for CETH's text collection because it is scholarly in nature yet has potentially wide use both for research and instruction, not only in literature but also in history, sociology, and related disciplines. It has been designed for many potential uses from printing to searching and browsing, and performing comparative studies and thus uses TEI SGML.

Maintaining material in different formats, which other repositories have done, creates a substantial overhead on the text management without much attendant benefit for users. A full archiving service for all electronic texts is not cost-effective, particularly given the state of many existing texts, which are not well documented and not proofread. Material in many different formats would require conversion to SGML, which is time-consuming and costly, or the provision and support of many different software programs to handle the texts. Material that is stored in a database format (e.g., dBase, Paradox, Advanced Revelation, and other relational database software) is even more problematic, because the database software package is needed to access the data, and it is often not easy to extract the data in the form it went in. Being selective, of course, raises the question of what to select, but this seems to be little different from any other collection development policy.

In the long-term, access via the network is the most effective way for texts to reach a wide audience with as much convenience and flexibility as possible. This method of access is already easy for many users and will become easier as the national information highway develops. It places no geographical restrictions on the use of the texts so that they are accessible to scholars and institutions anywhere within the United States and beyond. By joining the consortium, institutions that have more limited resources in their libraries will be able to provide their faculty and students with a broader range of material, accessible on their own campuses, without the need for substantial local support and maintenance. We envision a time when it will be just as normal for scholars to use the network to access full-text databases as it is for them now to retrieve bibliographic databases and e-mail.

Network access allows many more texts to be delivered, with the potential to use a broad range of different kinds of software, which is essential for dealing with the complex intellectual problems of scholarly texts. It also provides CETH with better control over the texts and the means to update them centrally without the need to send out new versions individually to many different users. For network access CETH is looking to much better facilities than are provided by ftp, listserv, gopher and the World Wide Web, all of which provide only a simple distribution mechanism. Two methods of access will be provided. The first will be for online searching. The second will permit downloading of texts for scholars to manipulate the texts, to serve their own needs. The first method of access will be important for classroom use and also for broad searches over a range of material. The second will enable scholars to use their own software, which is specific to their own individual requirements, and will thus permit greater flexibility in overall use.

The next stage is to link the Inventory to the Text Collection so that scholars can find the text they need in the Inventory and move straight from that to access the complete text. The Inventory will also point to other collections of text stored on other computers on the network and will provide access to them as part of the same software interface.

All CETH texts will be maintained in the TEI format and will be validated against the TEI DTDs before being made available. They will have a full TEI header that can be used for cataloging and other applications. SGML provides us with a means of encoding the complex features of scholarly texts in the humanities, but we also need to consider the types of searches that may be performed on these texts. These are not confined to searching for terms or content words as is the case with most retrieval systems in other disciplines. It is now widely accepted that studies of style or authorship can be best performed by a fine analysis of the use of common words or function words, and it is just these words that are not normally indexed in many systems. The spelling varies in older texts, and there is a need to bring together variant spellings in a more sophisticated way than can be performed by truncation. The analysis of names in historical texts can be problematic when it is not clear whether the same name refers to the same person or whether the same name has different spellings. Similarly, dates such as "in the reign of Nero" or "late 15th century" are not uncommon and need to be placed in the correct chronological sequence. The study of rhyme schemes in verse or morphological endings in an inflected language requires searches for words that end in certain letters. Some of these characteristics can be encoded within the text in SGML, but it is important also that the retrieval software recognizes them.

The real problem with almost all current retrieval systems is that they operate only on strings (sequences of letters). Boolean operators (AND, OR, NOT) have been the normal method of refining a string search ever since interactive text searching became available in the 1970s. Other methods of refining a search using weighted values, for example, also use only letter sequences as their fundamental unit. They provide limited facilities, when what the user is really looking for is concepts and ideas. The problem gets worse as larger and larger textbases become available and more unwanted material is retrieved. A combination of SGML tagging and better retrieval software can help to extract the knowledge from the information. One type of problem occurs when there are many instances of homographs (words which are spelled the same but with different meanings). For example, to look for all instances of "lead" (the metal), without finding "lead" (the verb) or "lead" (a piece of wire or string), in a Boolean search AND would be used to link the metal to other words with which it might associate (e.g., pencil or pipe). Word class tags embedded in a text in SGML syntax can be used to disambiguate or separate many homographs. In this case they would identify whether "lead" is a verb or a noun.

Word class tags on their own will not disambiguate the two meanings of the noun "lead," the metal and a piece of wire or string. To do this we also need a machine-readable dictionary from which a program can derive some semantic information about a word. The dictionary would provide, for example, all those words that are frequently close to "lead" (the metal) and would also indicate the environment or domain in which the metal lead can be used. We can see how this can help us move towards concept-based searching. The TEI's recommendations for dictionary encoding assume this as one use of a dictionary. The starting point is an electronic version of a printed dictionary, which then is converted into a lexical database in which the meanings are structured hierarchically. The dictionary can be considered a dynamic object and thus be updated with new information about meanings or word usage. These techniques are now used mostly on modern English, but they could easily be extended to other languages and to use historical dictionaries. For example, an electronic version of Liddell and Scott's *Lexicon of Classical Greek* linked to a version of the *Thesaurus Linguae Graecae* with morphological and word class tagging would provide much more sophisticated retrieval facilities than are currently possible by searching only for sequences of letters.

At present the most widely used software for searching SGML-tagged text in the academic environment seems to be PAT from the Open Text Corporation of Waterloo, Ontario. PAT is essentially a fast string searching program that operates on tagged text. It was designed initially for searching the *New Oxford English Dictionary* and early versions of it do not require the tags within the text to conform to SGML syntax in terms of a DTD. The current version handles SGML attributes in a very simple fashion. Several different user interfaces exist for PAT, of which the easiest to use are on machines that not many humanities scholars have on their desktops today. Dynatext from Electronic Book Technologies of Providence, Rhode Island, shows more promise than PAT in many ways, because it accepts any document in valid SGML syntax and is able to handle SGML attributes fully.

We also recognize that some scholars will wish to download texts for their own use, either for printing or for use with their own applications software. Sufficient information about the SGML tags will be provided for this, and we expect the tagging to be used to produce typographic features in the printed text, which makes it much easier to read than the screen or printer fonts that are in normal use. For example, there are several programs already in existence that convert SGML tags to the format used by the TeX typesetting program, and the capability for handling SGML is being introduced in some word processors. Appropriate security mechanisms will need to be developed to prevent unauthorized downloading and to maintain the integrity of the texts.

Educational Programs and Support Services

Educational programs and information services are needed to provide essential support for the Inventory and Text Collection. CETH has a newsletter and an electronic bulletin board ceth@pucc. CETH also organizes an annual two-week summer seminar "Electronic Texts: Methods and Tools" at Princeton each year. The first seminar in August 1992 was co-sponsored by the Centre for Computing in the Humanities, University of Toronto, and was attended by thirty participants, seven of whom were from abroad. The focus of the seminars is practical and methodological, concerned with the demonstrable benefits of using electronic texts in teaching and research, the typical problems one encounters and how to solve them, and the ways in which software fits or can be adapted to methods common to the humanities. Discussions on text creation, markup, retrieval, presentation, and analysis prepare the participants for extensive hands-on experience with software packages such as MTAS, Micro-OCP, Tact, and Collate. Systems of markup, from ad hoc schemes to the systematic approach of the Text Encoding Initiative, are surveyed and considered. Participants are given the opportunity to work on a coherent project. The seminar also includes presentations on specific topics or research projects as well as on the role of the library in electronic texts.

Conclusion

It seems, then, that enough lessons have been learned from the last thirty years for us to be able to create electronic texts that will be substantially more useful than the ones compiled years ago. Procedures have been devised for documenting texts, and the development of an SGML-based tagging scheme for the humanities addresses many scholarly concerns and provides a sound basis for further work. For the future, the real challenge lies in the provision of better software tools for intellectual access to the texts. In effect, we have progressed only little in the last twenty years in terms of more sophisticated retrieval systems that really help us to extract the knowledge from the information. CETH is planning the Text Collection and access mechanisms with the future in mind so that we can experiment with providing more sophisticated intellectual access once the basic procedures for using the Text Collection have been established. We plan to conduct research on the uses and users of these activities and research projects, which are supported within CETH or to which CETH is linked and which will provide testbeds within which software can be evaluated and new methodologies developed. From what we learn from this research, we will be able to identify more clearly what else is needed to provide high-quality electronic scholarly resources in the humanities and then work together with the members of our consortium to meet these needs.

References

Boguraev, B. and E. J. Briscoe, eds. *Computational Lexicography for Natural Language Processing*. London: Longman, 1989.

Burrows, J. F. *Computation into Criticism: A Study of Jane Austen's Novels and an Experiment in Method*. Oxford: Oxford University Press, 1987.

Fawcett, Heather J. *The PAT User Guide*. Waterloo: University of Waterloo Centre for the NOED, April 1989.

Hockey, Susan. *A Guide to Computer Applications in the Humanities*. Baltimore: Johns Hopkins, 1980.

Hockey, Susan. *The ACH-ACL-ALLC Text Encoding Initiative: An Overview*. TEI Document Number TEI J16, available from the file-server of TEI-L@UICVM.

Hockey, Susan and Nancy Ide, series eds., I. Lancashire, guest ed. *Research in Humanities Computing I*. Oxford: Oxford University Press, 1991.

Katzen, May, ed. *Scholarship and Technology in the Humanities*. British Library Research Series. London: Bowker-Saur, 1991.

Lancashire, Ian, ed. *Humanities Computing Yearbook 2*. Oxford: Oxford University Press, 1991.

Mylonas, E. 1992. "An Interface to Classical Greek Civilisation." *Journal of the American Society for Information Science* 43:192–201.

Neuman, M., ed. *The Georgetown University Catalogue of Projects in Electronic Text*. Center for Text and Technology, Academic Computer Center, Georgetown University, 1991.

Oxford Text Archive. *Shortlist of Machine-Readable Texts Held at Oxford*. Oxford: Oxford University Computing Services, 1992.

Sperberg-McQueen, C. M. 1991. "Text in the Electronic Age: Textual Study and Text Encoding with Examples from Medieval Texts." *Literary and Linguistic Computing* 6:34–46.

Sperberg-McQueen, C. M. and Lou Burnard, eds. *Guidelines for Electronic Text Encoding and Interchange*. TEI P3, Chicago and Oxford, May 1994.

Sutherland, Kathryn. 1990. "A Guide Through the Labyrinth: Dickens' Little Dorrit as Hypertext." *Literary and Linguistic Computing* 5:305–309.

TLG Newsletter. Thesaurus Linguae Graecae Project, University of California, Irvine, California.

Current and Future Trends in Network-Based Electronic Journals and Publishing

Michael Strangelove
Publisher
The Internet Business Journal
Ontario, Canada

I n December 1967 the Star Trek episode, "The Trouble with Tribbles," aired for the first time. That now classic episode opened with a scene that had Chief Engineer Scotty sitting at a computer terminal and looking at a full-colour, graphic image with text. Captain Kirk walked by and asked Scotty what he was doing. Scotty replied that he was "just keeping up with the trade journals." More than twenty-five years later, constellation-class starships are nowhere in sight, but we do have the global dissemination of electronic journals and newsletters. Within the global computer network, graphics and colour are available through the World Wide Web. Further, it is now possible to retrieve an electronic newsletter and read it in Mandarin script on a personal computer with the aid of a text-display utility.

Where are we in the history of network-distributed electronic serials and where are we headed in the near future? What trends in network-based electronic publishing can we expect to see develop over the next few years? These are some of the questions that this chapter will address.

What is the Net?

The Net, as it is often referred to, is the global computer network of networks that includes Bitnet, Internet, and affiliated research and education networks. This global network of networks contains millions of freely retrievable files and programs in thousands of ftp sites. It connects well over thirty million people, most major universities, and more than 1,100 computerized library catalogs. It should be noted that for the majority of networked individuals, use of the Net is entirely free.[1] Two of the main features of the academic Net are the capability to send and receive e-mail and the ability to archive text and program files on what is known as listserv and ftp fileservers.[2] These archives are then accessible from almost any point within the global Net.

The Directory of Electronic Journals and Newsletters

From 1991–1993 I tracked the growth of networked electronic journals and contributed that information to the *Directory of Electronic Journals and Newsletters.*[3] This directory is published annually by the Association of Research Libraries (ARL). As an indicator of the growth in electronic journals, we can compare the contents of several successive editions of the *Directory.* The first edition (1991) included 517 entries of which 110 were electronic journals and newsletters. The third edition (1993) listed over 200 electronic serials with description, subscription and back issue information, as well as a contact address for further queries. The fifth edition (1995) contains entries for nearly 2,500 scholarly lists and 675 electronic journals, newsletters, and related titles such as newsletter-digests. These figures for the fifth edition represent an increase of over 40 percent since the fourth edition of April 1994 and a 450 percent increase since the first edition of July 1991.[4]

When it began, the *Directory of Electronic Journals and Newsletters* represented a unique experiment in not-for-profit publishing by allowing the author to maintain the copyright to the electronic text and permitting the electronic version to remain freely accessible through the Net. ARL's implementation of this project demonstrated that it is possible to maintain network-accessible texts of print publications without undertaking a financial loss and without removing ownership of the text from the author. If such a model were aggressively pursued on a large scale by a consortium of learned societies and university presses, then libraries could stand to benefit by dramatically reduced acquisitions costs, and scholars would benefit by greater control over their intellectual production.

The *Religious Studies Publications Journal—CONTENTS*

The work of documenting the existence and growth of electronic serials led to two other related projects, one of which was the creation of an all electronic, network-distributed journal for religious studies known as the *Religious Studies Publications Journal—CONTENTS* (ISSN: 1188-5734).[5] This was an experimental journal that was intended to explore the potential of the Net as a vehicle for the dissemination and archiving of publication information and research material in religious studies and related fields. One of the primary functions of the *Religious Studies Publications Journal—CONTENTS*, also known as the CONTENTS Project, was to provide a central source of information on network-accessible resources for religious studies. Subscribers were notified of new electronic documents and were encouraged to contribute bibliographies, works in progress, course syllabi, theses and dissertations, and related material to the journal's ftp and listserv archives. This included electronic serial disseminated book and journal table of contents, ordering information, and reviews of both new books and journal articles. The journal also archived electronic versions of publishers' catalogs.

The *Religious Studies Publications Journal—CONTENTS* received funding from the American Academy of Religion to expand its ftp-accessible archive to a capacity of one gigabyte. This allowed it to make network-accessible the equivalent of approximately 100,000 pages of text. This also allowed the journal to archive a significant collection of so-called grey literature such as material produced by religious studies research centers throughout the world as well as complete theses and dissertations. One of the objectives of this experimental project was to provide a global point of electronic dissemination for research material such as theses, dissertations, major research papers, and bibliographies which are subject to limited distribution, often archived in awkward mediums such as microfiche, and are frequently unpublished.

By the end of its first year of operation (1992–1993), the *Religious Studies Publications Journal—CONTENTS* had over 1,000 subscribers in thirty countries. This journal had already archived via ftp the first complete thesis to be made available in electronic text on the Net as Postscript and WordPerfect files. In less than six months the *CONTENTS* Project archived on the Net over fourteen new bibliographies produced by the department of religious studies, University of Ottawa, which represented 450 pages of research material that would otherwise have been unpublished.

Combined electronic journals and ftp archives will play a leading role in reshaping the way in which scholarly material is disseminated and accessed by the next generation of networked researchers. The speed and impact of the changing technologies on academic institutions should not be underestimated. When I was in college, only one student had what was then a very expensive IBM desktop computer. Now more than fifty percent of the students at the University of Toronto have their own computer and some universities automatically supply every new student with one. Because the growth rate of the Internet and other computer networks is far greater than the growth rate of desktop computing, it will take a while for the full impact of the Net to be felt. Yet, there will soon come a point of convergence between the spread of desktop computing and the spread of the Net itself. This convergence will be characterized by pervasive network connectivity and dominant computer literacy among the next generation of faculty within academia. At this point we will begin to see the full realization of the virtual library and the global university without walls.

The Electric Mystic's Guide to the Internet

The experience of creating a network-distributed serial led to the challenge of documenting all existing network-accessible resources for religious studies and related fields. This document was titled *The Electric Mystic's Guide to the Internet: A Complete Bibliography of Networked Electronic Documents, Online Conferences, Serials, Software and Archives Relevant to Religious Studies.*[6] *The Electric Mystic's Guide* was a non-technical survey of all major documents, archives, and services relevant to religious studies and related fields that were freely available through the Net. This included networked papers, reviews, book notes, dissertations, major sacred texts, software programs, e-mail address collections, general information files, data banks, electronic journals, newsletters, online discussion groups, specialized commercial and public networks, and relevant networked organizations, associations, institutions, and companies.

The *Electric Mystic's Guide* is freely available on the Net as low ASCII, Postscript, and WordPerfect files. That it is at all possible to write almost 200 pages of documentation on network-accessible resources just in religious studies alone is a clear indication of the absolutely enormous size and growth rate of the academic computer networks.

Necessary Resources for Electronic Publication

If they are to succeed and survive over time, network-based electronic publishing projects require the support of local universities as well as learned societies. The American Academy of Religion gave financial support to the CONTENTS Project and to at least one other religious studies electronic serial. Support from learned societies is essential in a time when many humanities departments can barely afford to replace the toner cartridges in their laser printers. The support of Scholars Press for the print publication of the *Electric Mystic's Guide* represented a proactive stance that enabled the discipline to widely disseminate a basic directory of network resources in religious studies and thereby fostered further participation and development of the medium.

National and publicly supported research organizations must adopt policies that support network-based archives and do not separate the financial support of research from the dissemination of results. It is not unheard of to discover that the results of publicly funded research are seldom disseminated beyond the department that received the initial project funding. With disk space becoming less expensive, free network-based dissemination of federally funded material should be factored into funding allocations and made a mandatory prerequisite to actually receiving project funding at all. With the rise of the global Net and the favourable economics of university-based e-mail and electronic archives, research and publication need no longer be separated within the structure of funding policies.

Along with the support of learned societies, networked-based publishing projects also naturally require the support of a local university. I have been fortunate and have experienced the full cooperation of the computing and communication services of both the University of Ottawa and Carleton University. This support has been in the form of free e-mail use and helpful support staff. The ability to create listserv lists (online conferences) as needed is also essential. Mainframe ftp fileserver space has been provided at a cost that is actually less than the cost of an equivalent desktop computer. It is the humanities that will be at the forefront of network-based electronic publishing by virtue of the gradual disappearance of their journals and monograph publishers. Universities must begin mandating their computing services to provide sizable computing and Internet resources at costs that the poorest humanities department can afford if they wish to ensure that their departments can adjust to the coming disappearance of university presses and the shift to network-based scholarly communication and publishing.

Current State of Electronic Serials

Any discussion of networked electronic journals requires a keen sense of historical perspective. The desktop computer has been around for a little more than a decade and has become increasingly affordable only in the last few years. The Internet is about a decade old, and its exploding use is a recent phenomenon. Electronic journals began in the late 1980s, and the majority of electronic serials are less than four years old. While there can be no doubt that the global Net and computer-mediated communication and publishing carry absolutely staggering implications, it must be kept in mind that this technology-based system is still in its infancy. Speculation on where the Net is headed and what events will overtake network electronic publishing are, at this point, entirely tentative and eschatological in nature. Having said that, here are a few observations about the present and near future of electronic serials.

The future of electronic serials is largely unknown for the following reasons. We will likely see the Internet become increasingly commercialized over the next decade. This probably means increased traffic and technical problems as well as the possibility of a flood of junk mail. These two factors could threaten the academic nature of the Net and thus change it from being primarily a research and education forum into a business and sales forum. Along with the commercialization of the Net will come privatization, which will mean increased costs and perhaps a drop in the number of participating institutions in an increasingly weakening global economy. With these uncertainties in mind, it is best to keep the focus on what is presently available and possible in the area of networked publishing.

Distribution Methods

Electronic serials are distributed generally in one of two fashions. Subscribers are either sent the entire issue via e-mail or they receive a message that lists available articles and provides the file name of these articles and retrieval instructions. Sometimes subscribers are given the option of receiving the entire issue or just the table of contents.

Back issues of electronic serials are almost always archived on listserv or ftp fileservers and are freely available. The method of direct distribution of electronic serials has two main limitations, size and character set. Files that are too large will overload many user's mailboxes. Many people find files over 1,000 lines in length to be annoying and difficult to handle. Also, files sent directly as e-mail will be limited to low ASCII text. Low ASCII text includes only Aa to Zz and 1–9 and 0 along with a few other miscellaneous "safe" characters. Also, low ASCII eliminates many languages as well as scientific notation and graphics.[7]

Most electronic journals are accessible over the Internet without having a subscription. The Library of Congress and the Committee on Institutional Cooperation have extensive files of electronic publications which can be searched and downloaded from their gopher servers. Selected titles can also be found on various academic library catalogs or campus-wide information systems.

Electronic Serial Format Varieties

The main format that electronic serials are disseminated in is low ASCII. While there are a number of experiments with SGML, hypertext, HyperCard Stacks, TeX, and Postscript, low ASCII will nonetheless continue to be the primary format of electronic serials until its eventual replacement by UNICODE (a multilanguage universal replacement for low ASCII that will become pervasive). We will see a variety of sophisticated uses of integrated audio, visual, and graphical formats that take advantage of the leading edge of technology, but these will have a limited impact on overall trends until more users have the necessary connections and suitable front-end user interfaces such as Mosaic, Netscape, etc. The more complex solutions to the low ASCII barrier tend to demand more from the end user who simply desires to quickly access an issue or article. High-tech innovations will therefore have little impact on overall trends until their required hardware platforms are inexpensive and pervasive.[8]

The Immediate Future of Electronic Serials

The end of this decade will see anywhere from 5,000 to 500,000 network-accessible electronic serials available. A certain unknown percentage of these will be charging subscription rates, but the majority will continue to be freely accessible. In the coming few years we should see the following main trends in electronic journals.

1. Publishing houses will maintain network-accessible archives of their catalogs and will make a selection of their material available over the Net through World Wide Web sites. Mecklermedia was the first publisher to do this. Through their home page (http://www.mecklerweb.com), users can access a variety of information and services, including online ordering.

2. This trend will be followed by a parallel development that will see print journals offering condensed electronic versions of their issues on the Net. These condensed network-distributed versions will include such information as the issue table of contents, abstracts, the editorial and a lead article, and perhaps a few reviews or book notes. The intent will be to entice further print subscriptions and to encourage scholars to order entire issues or selected articles via the Net for a fee. This will occur with increasing frequency as we see a move away from whole document purchasing to selected chapter and article purchasing, facilitated via table of contents and abstract dissemination through the Net. Publishers will be forced to find innovative network-based marketing strategies in response to the continued massive serials cutbacks that we are beginning to witness at a growing number of universities. One notable example of this trend is *Academe This Week* which includes among its features news items, booklists and job postings from *The Chronicle of Higher Education.*

3. The third trend will be the widespread duplication of existing print newsletters and bulletins into electronic copies for dissemination via the Net. There will be an absolute flood of electronic versions of newsletters and bulletins on the Net as institutions and organizations become aware of the massive potential to reach remote students and

members. As most academic and institutional newsletters and bulletins are produced not for profit but for publicity purposes, they will find that there is ample justification for the relatively inexpensive process of creating an electronic version.

4. There will be the creation of large table of contents databases. We will certainly witness various consortia of university presses, learned associations, and libraries creating enormous table of content, abstract, and ordering information databases that will be freely accessible via the Net. This is still a few years away, but eventually we will see the creation of what could be called the global village's bookstore.

5. We will see more electronic journals picked up by traditional publishers and reproduced in print and other formats as well. This trend is reflected in the effort by Oxford University Press to provide back issues of the electronic journal *Postmodern Culture* (ISSN: 1053-1920) which began in 1990, on diskette and microfiche. This activity represents a transitional phase in the development of electronic journals. Eventually it will be clearly counterproductive to duplicate every quality electronic journal as a print or microform journal, as this will only further burden shrinking acquisition budgets. Because universities will remain print-based organizations for quite some time to come, dual electronic-print serials will flourish, but they will represent a transitional phenomenon in the longer sweep of history.

6. Finally, there will be the ongoing trend of new, creative, and exploratory all-electronic academic and popular journals appearing on the Net. This trend will be accompanied by the retrospective conversion of many humanities serials into freely accessible back issue networked databases. The rate of appearance of new electronic academic journals will be considerably increased once the medium gains acceptance and integration into existing indexes, peer reviews, and promotion mechanisms. While a multitude of issues and technical problems need to be addressed and overcome before the complete legitimation of this new medium, its full maturity and acceptance is, in the end, only a matter of time.

One of the primary forces that will motivate change and innovation on the Net will be the realization in all commercial sectors that the Net represents the single largest audience outside of television. Such a phenomenon will not be able to resist the penetration of market interests. That which remains to be seen is to what degree not-for-profit initiatives will be able to stand against coalitions of market interests seeking to carve the Net into commercial territories. The result of this coming struggle between supporters of free access to publicly funded information and commercial interests will determine the shape of scholarly communication well into the next century and beyond.

Universities and their libraries and learned societies have an opportunity to shape and influence these trends in network-based publishing to their advantage. Only time will tell if this historic frontier will become an environment for collective, creative development or market-driven exploitation by private interests. The following decade will reveal which is more capable of rapid, innovative and self-interested adaptation, not-for-profit academic interests or free-market forces of profit and privatization.

Conclusion

If these present and future trends have not been entirely overstated, then libraries are faced with a host of issues that have arisen in light of the arrival by the end of the decade of perhaps 500,000 electronic serials. How will this new and potentially enormous and pervasive medium be integrated into existing structures of information organization and brokering? Libraries will be the key to the success or failure of electronic scholarly publishing. With proper proactive management, the success of this new medium will benefit both libraries and the academic community. However, if the academic community and libraries fail to take the initiative in the development of this new medium, then we will be faced with a budgetary and organizational nightmare that may lead to an increased drain on declining acquisition budgets. This will take the form of a growing demand for both electronic and print subscriptions to the same expensive commercial serial.

A fundamental problem that universities face today is that while they are the sole creators of academic knowledge, they have largely abandoned the role of the final legitimation of that knowledge to the realm of publishers. If libraries, universities, and learned societies work together to produce, archive, disseminate, and legitimate electronic, network-accessible, "in-house" publishing, then we will see the present extreme dependency on the commercial publishing industry slowly evaporate as we move towards the networked "university without walls" of the next century.

Ann Okerson, director of the Office of Scientific and Academic Publishing of the Association of Research Libraries, has noted that for the first time in over 200 years, the paper scholarly journal can be supplanted, or at least, supplemented in a significant way by the rise of network-based electronic journals and that this may lead to a new type of scholarly discourse.[9] I think that a paradigm shift in the process of scholarly discourse is on the horizon and that this will be accompanied by a fundamental shift in the technological basis of academic communication and publishing.

The urban communication infrastructure is slowly being converted from copper wire to fibre optics. We will soon see the majority of urban centers interconnected through community-based Freenets that are linked via telnet and e-mail to the global Net. The computer industry will shortly introduce affordable laptops and palmtops and, whereas my generation was the last to carry sliderules to high school classes, we will eventually see widespread notebook computing within colleges and universities.

At some not too distant point in time, there will be a convergence between the growth of community telecomputing in the form of Freenets, the maturity of a pervasive global Net, and a significant drop in the cost of entrance-level desktop and notebook computers. The prior existence and maturation of scholarly electronic journals and the proliferation of network-accessible publications will provide the foundation for making the fruits of academic research and writing widely available to the global citizens of the emergent Electric Gaia. Librarians are certainly destined to play a key role in disseminating the publicly funded and freely accessible electronic scholarly information when, for the first time in history, we will have a seamless interface between the university and the community. This university-community interface will take the form of a supernetwork of community Freenets that are linked to the larger academic Net and thereby have direct access to the growing wealth of electronic information resources created by and for all peoples. Hopefully the current trends in network-based electronic publishing will continue in such a way that will foster the speedy arrival of such an information system.

Endnotes

1. This is no longer true as of late 1995 because the number of commercial users of the Net has surpassed the number of academic users.

2. Since the development of the World Wide Web, the user of listserv and FTP fileserves has declined.

3. *The Directory of Electronic Journals and Newsletters*, 5th edition, is available on the Internet at: gopher ccat.sas.upenn.edu under the listing for Electronic Publications and Resources.

4. Ann Okerson, "ARL 5th Edition of Directory of Electronic Publications Available." Press Release (18 May 1995).

5. *The Religious Studies Publications Journal—CONTENTS* is available on the Internet on the Library of Congress (LC Marvel): gopher marvel.loc.gov under Global Electronic Library, Philosophy and Religion Journals.

6. *The Electric Mystic's Guide to the Internet* is available on the Internet on the Library of Congress (LC MARVEL): gopher marvel.loc.gov under Global Electronic Library, Philosophy and Religion, Guides to Philosophy and Religion Resources on the Internet.

7. The widespread use of mime-compliant e-mail programs and the World Wide Web itself has resolved many graphical issues.

8. In the end, the solution has come in the form of software such as Mosaic and Netscape, World Wide Web browsers.

9. Ann Okerson, "The Electronic Journal: What, Whence and When?" *The Public-Access Computer Systems Review* 2, 1 (1992): 5–24.

Editor's Note

When Michael Strangelove wrote this chapter, he was a Social Sciences and Humanities Research Council Doctoral Fellow, Department of Religious Studies, University of Ottawa. The chapter has since been updated by the editor.

Contributors

SUSAN HOCKEY is the Director of the Center for Electronic Texts in the Humanities, which is operated jointly by Rutgers and Princeton Universities, New Jersey.

GEORGE S. MACHOVEC, formerly the Head of Library Technology and Systems at Arizona State University, Tempe, Arizona, is currently the Technical Coordinator for the Colorado Alliance of Research Libraries, Denver, Colorado.

BERNARD A. MARGOLIS is the Director of the Pikes Peak Library District, Colorado Springs, Colorado.

MAURICE MITCHELL is the Assistant Director, Internetworking Services and Planning System Computing Services for the Universities and Community Colleges of Nevada.

DENNIS NICHOLSON is the Library Systems Officer at Strathclyde University in Glasgow, Scotland.

BARBARA G. RICHARDS is the Associate Director of Libraries at Carnegie Mellon University, Pittsburgh, Pennsylvania.

LAVERNA M. SAUNDERS is Dean of the Library and Instructional and Learning Support at Salem State College, Salem, Massachusetts. Also, she is the moderator for the Virtual Library track at the annual Computers in Libraries conference.

CONNIE STOUT is the Director of the Texas Education Network (TENET) which is based in the Texas Education Agency, Austin, Texas.

MICHAEL STRANGELOVE is the publisher of the *Internet Business Journal* and former Social Sciences and Humanities Research Council Doctoral Fellow in the Department of Religious Studies, University of Ottawa, Ontario, Canada.

Index

Other Books of Interest from Information Today, Inc.

Key Guide to Electronic Resources: Health Sciences
Edited by Lee Hancock ($39.50/494pp/ISBN 1-57387-001-3)

Key Guide to Electronic Resources: Agriculture
Edited by Wilfred Drew ($39.50/124pp/ISBN 1-57387-000-5)

CD-ROM Finder, 6th Edition 1995
Kathleen Hogan and James Shelton, Editors ($69.50/520pp/ISBN 0-938734-86-5)

The Electronic Classroom: A Handbook for Education in the Electronic Environment
Edited by Erwin Boschmann ($42.50/240pp/ISBN 0-938734-89-X)

Document Delivery Services: Issues and Answers
By Eleanor Mitchell and Sheila Walters ($42.50/333pp/ISBN 1-57387-003-X)

Multimedia in Higher Education
By Helen Carlson and Dennis R. Falk ($42.50/176pp/ISBN 1-57387-002-1)

CD-ROM for Library Users: A Guide to Managing and Maintaining User Access
Paul Nicholls and Pat Ensor, Editors ($39.50/138 pp/ISBN 0-938734-95-4)

Electronic Image Communications: A Guide to Networking Image Files
By Richard J. Nees ($39.50/95pp/ISBN 0-938734-87-3)

Navigating the Networks
Deborah Lines Anderson, Thomas J. Galvin, & Mark D. Giguere, Editors
($29.95/255pp/ISBN 0-938734-85-7)

Challenges in Indexing Electronic Text and Images
Raya Fidel, Trudi Bellardo Hahn, Edie Rasmussen, and Philip Smith, Editors
($39.50/316pp/ISBN 0-938734-76-8)

K-12 Networking: Breaking Down the Walls of the Learning Environment
By Doris Epler ($39.50/190pp/ISBN 0-938734-94-6)

INNOPAC: A Reference Guide to the System
By Terry Ballard ($39.50/216pp/ISBN 1-57387-015-3)

ProCite in Libraries: Applications in Bibliographic Database Management
Edited by Deb Renee Biggs ($39.50/221pp/ ISBN 0-938734-90-3)

Information Management for the Intelligent Organization
By Chun Wei Choo ($39.50/255pp/ISBN 1-57387-018-8)

Government CD-ROMs: A Practical Guide to Searching Electronic Documents Databases
Edited by John Maxymuk ($47.50/350pp/ISBN 0-88736-887-5)

Automated Library Systems: A Librarians Guide and Teaching Manual
By Beverly K. Duval and Linda Main ($40.00/288pp/ISBN 0-88736-873-5)

Library Technology Consortia: Case Studies in Design and Cooperation
Edited by Jerry Kuntz ($42.50/165pp/ISBN 0-88736-886-7)

The Virtual Library: Visions and Realities
Edited by Laverna Saunders ($37.50/180pp/ISBN 0-88736-860-3)

Electronic Journal Literature: Implications for Scholars
By Jan Olsen ($25.00/100pp/ISBN 0-88736-925-1)

Small Project Automation for Libraries and Information Centers
By Jane Mandelbaum ($35.00/350pp/ISBN 0-88736-731-3)

CD-ROM Book Index
Edited by Ann Niles ($39.50/207pp/ISBN 0-938734-98-9)

Proceedings of the 16th National Online Meeting, May 2-4, 1995
($55.00/448pp/ISBN 1-57387-004-8)

Annual Review of Information Science and Technology, Volume 30
Edited by Martha Williams ($98.50/525pp/ISBN 1-57387-019-6)

To order directly from the publisher, include $3.95 postage and handling for the first book ordered and $3.25 for each additional book. Catalogs also available upon request.

Information Today, Inc., 143 Old Marlton Pike, Medford, NJ 08055, (609)654-6266